12 R/5.

GUIDE TO THE INDUSTRIAL RELATIONS ACT 1971

By

NORMAN M. SELWYN,

LL.M., Dip. Econ. (Oxon.), A.C.I.S., Barrister,
Lecturer in Law at the University of
Aston in Birmingham

LONDON
BUTTERWORTHS
1971

ENGLAND: BUTTERWORTH & CO. (PUBLISHERS) LTD.
                LONDON: 88 Kingsway, WC2B 6AB
AUSTRALIA: BUTTERWORTH & CO. (AUSTRALIA) LTD.
                SYDNEY: 586 Pacific Highway, Chatswood,
                NSW 2067
                MELBOURNE: 343 Little Collins Street, 3000
                BRISBANE: 240 Queen Street, 4000
CANADA: BUTTERWORTH & CO. (CANADA) LTD.
                TORONTO: 14 Curity Avenue 374
NEW ZEALAND: BUTTERWORTH & CO. (NEW ZEALAND) LTD.
                WELLINGTON: 26–28 Waring Taylor Street, 1
                AUCKLAND: 35 High Street, 1
SOUTH AFRICA: BUTTERWORTH & CO. (SOUTH AFRICA) (PTY.)
                LTD.
                DURBAN: 152-154 Gale Street

PREFACE

The object of this book is to provide a guide to the Industrial Relations Act 1971 for the benefit of company directors, management personnel, trade unionists and students (of law and industrial relations). The Act, which is probably one of the most controversial pieces of legislation passed by Parliament this century, is the result of a long series of events, with heated arguments, differing opinions, bitter disputes and political manœuvring. It may well be that it is not the last word on the subject.

I have not sought to write a treatise on the political, sociological, industrial or historical significance of the introduction of the philosophy of law into the industrial relations system. The debate has been going on now for a number of years, and will, no doubt, continue. There is no shortage of material, ranging from the Donovan Report to the Consultative Document, Fair Deal at Work to In Place of Strife. *Quot homines, tot sententiæ.* Nor have I attempted to assess the merits or de-merits of any particular proposal contained in the Act, or commented on any particular omission. It seems to me that a discourse on these lines would probably require another book altogether, and I am not sure of my qualifications to enter on such an enterprise. For although I started my working life on the factory floor, and have always been a keen trade unionist, I am not persuaded that all change is undesirable, or that the future of the industrial relations system in this country is a suitable subject for the political hustings. Perhaps the most significant feature of the arguments of those who opposed "the Bill" was the omission of any constructive alternative proposals worthy of serious consideration, and until such ideas are formulated in detail, one tends to get bogged down in an argument about conflicting political philosophies, rather than the realities of industrial relations. In any case, the Act is now part of the law of the land, and for the moment, at any rate, it is necessary to study its provisions as they are, not as we think they are or think they ought to be.

Whether the legislation will be successful in achieving any particular object can now only be judged by time—assuming (which is doubtful) that there is agreement on what the desired objects are. But until we have had at least a few years' experience of the new institutional arrangements and the social and industrial consequences

v

of trying to bring a new rule of law into industrial relations, I would imagine that further disputation would tend to be unproductive. No doubt each and every reader of this book will have his own preconceived notions and prejudices, and I see little point in adding my own to the debate which has now finished in a book which is primarily designed to assist in the process of study.

I have tried to simplify certain provisions of the Act in order that they may be better understood and I trust that this has not resulted in any distortion. For example, whenever I have referred to something being an unfair industrial practice, I have generally not elaborated on attempts and threats to do (or not to do) the same thing. Sometimes it has been necessary to discuss the Act in the context of the existing law (e.g., the law relating to the legal enforceability of collective agreements), but by and large I have tried to avoid this and have treated the Act in isolation, mainly because I have a suspicion that the NIRC and the tribunals will try to start from fresh premises, and will build up a new body of jurisprudence untrammelled by previous legal authority. This, at any rate, would seem to me to be a sensible and desirable development, rather than attempting to shackle the growth of a new law by legal rules drawn (sometimes inappropriately) from other fields of human activity.

Some of the minor provisions of the Act have been left to be dealt with by other textbooks in their respective fields of study, and I have given them only a passing glance. In one or two places I have included a brief summary of existing legal rules which are unaffected by the Act, merely for the sake of convenience, for they are a relevant part of the whole picture.

The abbreviations NIRC, CIR and IAB have been used for National Industrial Relations Court, Commission on Industrial Relations and Industrial Arbitration Board. Also, I am conscious of a certain amount of repetition in the text, which has been necessary in order to avoid the constant use of "see *post*, page 00", or "see *ante*, page 00", etc. It is bad enough for a non-lawyer to have to wander through a series of connected references in the Act without having to do so in a book designed to explain it!

In certain respects, the language of the Act will be as unfamiliar to lawyers as it is to industrial relations practitioners. Thus, instead of a plaintiff issuing a writ against a defendant in respect of a tortious act arising out of a trade dispute, we may soon be reading about a complainant making a complaint against a respondent in respect of an unfair industrial practice arising out of an industrial dispute. The Act provides new remedies—an order directing the respondent to refrain from doing something, an order determining the rights of the complainant, an award of compensation, and so forth. Of course, any resemblance between these new remedies and an injunction, a declaratory judgment, and damages is purely co-incidental! Those who practice in industrial relations will have to familiarise themselves with a number of new concepts, including the agency shop, approved closed shop, bargaining agencies, and so forth. Now that legalism has replaced the voluntary system, the days of the (enthusiastic) amateur are over.

Several words of warning must be given. In the first place I have written as if the whole of the Act was immediately in force. In fact, the Secretary of State will bring it into operation gradually, and different times will be appointed (possibly with certain transitional provisions) for the various parts to become effective. Provisionally it is planned to open the office of the Chief Registrar of Trade Unions and Employers' Associations in October this year, which will enable the registration provisions to come into effect by November. The CIR will be reconstituted ready for its new role, and in December the NIRC will be set up. It will then be possible to bring into force all those provisions of the Act which deal with agency shops and approved closed shops, bargaining agencies, exclusion orders for dismissal procedures, presumptions relating to collective agreements, remedial action in respect of defective procedure, emergency procedure and appeals to the NIRC from the decisions of the Chief Registrar. The industrial tribunals are expected to be ready to cope with the increased volume of work early in 1972, and other sections of the Act will then be brought into effect, dealing with rights in respect of trade unionism, the modifications made to the Contracts of Employment Act, unfair dismissals, disclosure of information by employers to trade unions and employees, complaints against registered organisations, restrictions on certain types of legal proceedings and other unfair industrial practices. In order to ease the burden of work the Secretary of State will use his powers to restrict the application of certain provisions of the Act initially to undertakings with more than a specified number of employees. Secondly, I have, in certain sections, indicated my own views as to how particular provisions will be interpreted by the NIRC and tribunals. In these, I may well be wrong, but until legal authority is available, I can only stand by an opinion honestly held. Finally, in the event of any legal problem arising (whether real or academic) it is to be hoped that the reader will consult the Act itself (and where necessary, take competent advice), rather than rely on my (sometimes) simplified version. This book is designed to be a guide, not a Bible.

I am grateful to the publishers for their helpful co-operation at every stage of the production of this book.

The University of Aston   N. M. S.
Gosta Green,
Birmingham 4.
August 1971

TABLE OF CONTENTS

All references are to paragraph numbers.

CHAPTER FIVE. LEGAL REMEDIES

CHAPTER SIX. EMERGENCY PROCEDURES

CHAPTER SEVEN. INDIVIDUAL RIGHTS

CHAPTER EIGHT.   THE RIGHT TO STRIKE

INDEX

TABLE OF REFERENCES
TO
THE INDUSTRIAL RELATIONS ACT 1971

All references are to paragraph numbers.

xiii

xiv

TABLE OF REFERENCES TO THE ACT

TABLE OF CASES

In the following Table references are given where applicable to the English
and Empire Digest where a digest of the case will be found.
All references are to paragraph numbers.

A

xvii

PARA.

N

Nagle *v.* Fielden, [1966] 2 Q.B. 633; [1966] 1 All E.R. 689; [1966] 2 W.L.R. 1027; 110 Sol. Jo. 286, C.A.; Digest Cont. Vol. B 323 .. ..   [103]

National Coal Board *v.* Galley, [1958] 1 All E.R. 91; [1958] 1 W.L.R. 16; 102 Sol. Jo. 31, C.A.; Digest Cont Vol. A 463 ..   [261]

P

Piddington *v.* Bates, [1960] 3 All E.R. 660; [1961] 1 W.L.R. 162; 105 Sol. Jo. 110; Digest Cont. Vol. A 411 .. .. ..   [342]

Q

Quinn *v.* Leathem, [1901] A.C. 495; [1900–3] All E.R. Rep. 1; 70 L.J.P.C. 76; 85 L.T. 289; 65 J.P. 708; 50 W.R. 139; 17 T.L.R. 749, H.L.; 45 Digest (Repl.) 280 .. ..   [270]

R

Reynolds *v.* Shipping Federation, Ltd., [1924] 1 Ch. 28; [1923] All E.R. Rep. 383; 93 L.J. Ch. 70; 130 L.T. 341; 39 T.L.R. 710; 68 Sol. Jo. 61; 45 Digest (Repl.) 569   [273]

Rooks *v.* Barnard, [1964] A.C. 1129; [1964] 1 All E.R. 367; [1964] 2 W.L.R. 269; 108 Sol. Jo. 93; [1964] 1 Lloyd's Rep. 28, H.L.; Digest Cont. Vol. B 217 .. ..   [274], [376]

S

Scala Ballroom (Wolverhampton), Ltd. *v.* Ratcliffe, [1958] 3 All E.R. 220; [1958] 1 W.L.R. 1057; 102 Sol. Jo. 758, C.A.; 45 Digest (Repl.) 559 .. ..   [273]

South Wales Miners' Federation *v.* Glamorgan Coal Co., [1905] A.C. 239; [1904–7] All E.R. Rep. 211; 74 L.J.K.B. 525; 92 L.T. 710; 53 W.R. 593; 21 T.L.R. 441, H.L.; 45 Digest (Repl.) 306 .. ..   [174], [269]

Spring *v.* National Amalgamated Stevedores and Dockers Society, [1956] 2 All E.R. 221; [1956] 1 W.L.R. 585; 100 Sol. Jo. 401; [1956] 1 Lloyd's Rep. 331; 45 Digest (Repl.) 541 .. ..   [132]

Strafford (J. T.) & Son, Ltd. *v.* Lindley, [1965] A.C. 269; [1964] 3 All E.R. 102; [1964] 3 W.L.R. 541; 108 Sol. Jo. 636; [1964] 2 Lloyd's Rep. 133, H.L.; 45 Digest (Repl.) 310 .. ..   [181], [269]

T

Thomson (D. C.) & Co., Ltd. *v.* Deakin, [1952] Ch. 646; [1952] 1 T.L.R. 1397; affirmed, [1952] Ch. at p. 666; [1952] 2 All E.R. 361; [1952] 2 T.L.R. 105, C.A.; 45 Digest (Repl.) 562 ..   [181], [309]

Torquay Hotel Co., Ltd. *v.* Cousins, [1969] 2 Ch. 106; [1968] 3 All E.R. 43; [1968] 3 W.L.R. 540; 112 Sol. Jo. 668; affirmed, [1969] 2 Ch. at p. 123; [1969] 1 All E.R. 522; [1969] 2 W.L.R. 289; 113 Sol. Jo. 52, C.A.; Digest Cont. Vol. C. 561.. ..   [296]

Tyan *v.* Balmer, [1967] 1 Q.B. 1; [1966] 2 All E.R. 133; [1966] 2 W.L.R. 1181; 110 Sol. Jo. 129; Digest Cont. Vol. B 190 ..   [342]

W

White *v.* Kuzych, [1951] A.C. 585; [1951] 2 All E.R. 435; [1951] 2 T.L.R. 277; 95 Sol. Jo. 527, P.C.; 45 Digest (Repl.) 543 ..   [133]

CHAPTER ONE

INSTITUTIONAL ARRANGEMENTS

INTRODUCTORY PRINCIPLES

In order to understand how the system introduced by the Industrial Relations Act 1971 will work, it is necessary first to look at the organisational structure of the new institutions. By way of an introduction, section 1 states that the provisions of the Act shall have effect for the purpose of promoting good industrial relations in accordance with four general principles. These are:

(a) the principle of collective bargaining freely conducted on behalf of workers and employers and with due regard to the general interests of the community;

(b) the principle of developing and maintaining orderly procedures in industry for the peaceful and expeditious settlement of disputes by negotiation, conciliation or arbitration, with due regard to the general interests of the community;

(c) the principle of free association of workers in independent trade unions, and of employers in employers' associations, so organised as to be representative, responsible and effective bodies for regulating relations between employers and workers; and

(d) the principle of freedom and security for workers, protected by adequate safeguards against unfair industrial practices, whether on the part of employers or others. **[1]**

It is, to say the least, unusual for an Act of Parliament to begin with a statement of purpose and principles in this manner, but the section continues to say that with a view to fulfilling that purpose those principles shall be regarded as *guiding principles* by:

(a) the Secretary of State, the Commission on Industrial Rel ations the Registrar of Trade Unions and Employers' Associations (and his assistants) in the performance of their functions under the Act; and

(b) by the National Industrial Relations Court and the Industrial Tribunals, in the exercise of their jurisdiction conferred by the Act. **[2]**

Although it is possible to regard the four principles in section 1 as a set of platitudes (indeed, critics have taken the view that the rest of the Act is in conflict with those principles!), it is quite likely that reference will be made to them in cases of doubt. This is particularly so when considering how the NIRC will re-act, in practice, to its various tasks, for not all the provisions of the Act are either clear or reconcilable. Indeed, the section may even permit the NIRC to by-pass the doctrine of precedent (whereby a court is, generally speaking, bound by a decision of a higher court; decisions of a court of equal standing are of persuasive value only) if it should ever arise that the following of a precedent may result in a conflict with those principles.   [3]

Section 2 requires the Secretary of State to prepare a draft Code of Practice, which will contain such practical guidance as in his opinion would be helpful for the purpose of promoting good industrial relations. The Code must be drawn up bearing in mind:

(a) the need for those who manage undertakings to accept the primary responsibility for the promotion of good industrial relations; and

(b) the need to provide practical guidance with respect to the disclosure of information by employers, and the establishment of and maintenance of effective means of negotiation, consultation, and communication at all levels between those who manage undertakings and the workers employed in them.

The Code must be laid before Parliament within one year of the passing of the Act, and, if approved by resolution of each House, will be issued in the form so approved. The Code can be revised from time to time, in which case the Secretary of State must consult with the Trades Union Congress and the Confederation of British Industry before preparing the revised draft, and shall then submit a copy of the new draft to the CIR for their consideration and advice.
                                                                                  [4]

Section 4 provides that a failure on the part of any person to observe any provision in the Code shall not of itself render him liable to any proceedings, but, in any proceedings before the NIRC or an industrial tribunal:

(a) the Code shall be admissible in evidence; and

(b) any provision of the Code which the NIRC or the Industrial Tribunal considers to be relevant to any question arising in those proceedings shall be taken into account in determining the question.

The Code, therefore, will perform the role of a "Highway Code" of industrial relations—not legally binding in itself, but a guide to look at in order to establish the rights and duties of the various parties to the proceedings. It will be written in non-legal language, but it cannot be used to override the provisions of the Act. In so far as it is intended to be a guide to good industrial relations practice, it has been suggested that the Code, rather than the Act, will be in the forefront of the minds of management and workers' representatives. [5]

A. THE NATIONAL INDUSTRIAL RELATIONS COURT (Section 99 and 3rd Schedule)

This is to be a new branch of the High Court, and will consist of such judges as are nominated by the Lord Chancellor from among the members of the High Court and the Court of Appeal (plus one judge from the Court of Session, nominated by the Lord President), and lay members appointed by the Queen, on the joint recommendation of the Lord Chancellor and the Secretary of State. One of the nominated judges will be appointed to be the President of the Court. The lay members are to be appointed from persons who have special knowledge or experience of industrial relations. [6]

Lay members will normally be appointed for a term of not less than three years, and are eligible for re-appointment; they may resign at any time, and their appointment may be terminated by the Lord Chancellor and the Secretary of State on the ground of incapacity or misbehaviour. Temporary appointments may be made if a nominated or an appointed member is absent or unable to act. Lay members will sit as full members of the court, not as assessors. They will, therefore, be able to out-vote the judge, though, on questions of law, they will presumably follow his rulings. [7]

The court will have its central office in London, but may sit anywhere in Great Britain. It is likely to do this when this is more convenient to the parties in the case in question, for example, if there are large numbers of witnesses involved. The composition of the court will normally consist of the judge and not less than two, nor more than four appointed members, though with the consent of all the parties a case may be heard by the judge and one appointed member. In practice, it is expected that two appointed members will sit with the judge. [8]

Proceedings before the NIRC will be governed by rules to be made by the Lord Chancellor (after consultation with the Lord President of the Court of Session) and will include provisions to ensure that the parties to any proceedings may always avail themselves of the conciliation facilities. The NIRC will regulate its own procedure, and in this respect, the normal formalities attendant on a High Court hearing will be avoided as far as is appropriate; as the Solicitor General has said, there will not be any "Jacobean costumes to antiquate the atmosphere". A person may appear before the **NIRC** to argue a case on his own behalf, or he may be represented by counsel, or by a solicitor, or by a representative of his trade union (or employers' association, as the case may be) or by any other person whom he desires to represent him. The normal rules of evidence will not be binding on the court except in two special cases (i.e., appeals under sections 114 and 115) when it is thought that the complex legal issues will be such that the parties will engage counsel. The court will normally sit in public, but may sit in private:

(a) to hear evidence where the matters referred to are of such a nature that it is against the interests of national security to allow the evidence to be given in public; or

(b) any information which may be of a confidential nature.

The latter will include matters such as where the Official Secrets Act applies, or where the evidence was communicated to a witness in confidence, or where the evidence relates to an individual which may be seriously prejudicial to him, or evidence which may be prejudicial to the employer's business other than in respect of its effect of collective bargaining, or information obtained for the purpose of bringing or defending any legal proceedings, or, so far as the Crown is concerned, evidence, the disclosure of which would be contrary to the national interest. Anything communicated to the Registrar while the latter is investigating certain complaints (see section 82 (7)), or to a conciliation officer who is performing certain functions (see section 146 (6)) is not admissible in evidence without the consent of the person who made the communication. Thus the confidential nature of the relationship is preserved. **[9]**

The court may make an interim order at any stage of the proceedings, but not against a person unless all reasonable steps have been taken to secure that he knows of the interim order, and an opportunity is given to him to make representations relating to that application.[1] **[10]**

The court may order any party before it to pay the whole or part of the costs of any other party, if:

(a) the proceedings were unnecessary or vexacious or improper; or

(b) there has been unreasonable delay or unreasonable conduct in bringing or conducting the case.

Subject to this, the court will not be permitted to make any order as to costs or expenses, and the rule thus becomes that all parties must

---

[1] In other words, "ex parte" applications, whereby the court can grant an immediate, but temporary, order, in the absence of the other party to the dispute, are not, generally speaking, to be permitted in the NIRC.

pay their own. Legal aid, however, will be available in appropriate cases.   [11]

A complaint in respect of an unfair industrial practice (brought under section 101) or of a breach of duty by the employer (brought under section 102) must normally be presented within six months from the earliest time when the action to which the complaint relates came to the notice of the complainant (or would have done had he exercised due diligence), but an appropriate allowance of time may be made for any period during which the parties have availed themselves of the services of conciliation officers or other conciliation facilities. Generally speaking, the NIRC will decide issues on equitable principles, and any claim brought before the court will have to be well-founded in law and fact for the complainant to succeed. Thus, section 101 states that "if it considers to be just and equitable", the court will make certain awards, and the phrase is to be found in other sections. For example, if a strike breaks out because of intolerable working conditions, or because the employer has failed to provide adequate safety precautions, although the strike may amount to an unfair industrial practice, the amount of compensation which the employer will obtain will be reduced as the court thinks just and equitable, for the court will consider the extent to which the strike was caused or contributed to by the employer's own conduct in the matter. In an appropriate case, therefore, the court may be unwilling to make any award whatsoever.   [12]

Any award or compensation made by the NIRC shall have effect for the purpose of enforcement as if it were a judgment of the High Court.[2] It has similar powers in respect of the attendance and examination of witnesses, production of documents, etc., and can, if necessary, commit a person to prison for contempt of court.   [13]

The decisions of the NIRC on questions of fact will be final, but an appeal will lie to the Court of Appeal[3] on questions of law.   [14]

Jurisdiction of the court

The court, has a wide range of jurisdiction to deal with issues which arise out of the Act. We will state this jurisdiction here in brief; later chapters will expound the issues.   [15]

(a) *Agency shop agreements* (see Chapter 4)

If a trade union or joint negotiating panel desires an employer to enter into an agency shop agreement, and the employer refuses to do so, then either party may make an application to the NIRC. If satisfied that the application is properly made, the NIRC will send

---

[2] In Scotland, as a recorded decree arbital.
[3] In Scotland, the Court of Session.

the matter to the CIR for investigation. If the CIR consider that the matter ought to be dealt with under the sole bargaining agency provisions it shall report this to the NIRC, and proceed no further with the reference. Otherwise, the CIR will arrange for a ballot to be taken, and report the result to the NIRC and the other interested parties. If the ballot proves in favour of an agency shop agreement, it then becomes the duty of the employer to enter into such agreement, and carry it out. Failure to do so may mean that the trade union may make an application to the NIRC under section 102, which may make an order specifying the rights of the trade union, and/or an order directing the employer to fulfil that duty. If the result of the ballot is in the negative, the NIRC will make an order that no agency shop agreement shall operate there for two years, and no further application can be made during that period in respect of those employees,   [16]

Once an agency shop has been established, one-fifth of the employees covered by it may make an application to the NIRC for its revocation, though if the agreement was ordered by the NIRC in the first place, they must wait two years from the date of the order before they can do so. Again, the NIRC will request the CIR to arrange for a ballot to be taken, and the result will be reported as above. If the requisite majority have not voted in favour of the continuance of the agency shop, the NIRC will rescind the agreement, and no agency shop agreement can be entered into by the employer and trade union for two years in respect of those employees.   [17]

(b) *Approved closed shop agreements* (see Chapter 4)

An employer or an organisation of employers, and one or more trade unions may jointly make an application to the NIRC for permission to enter into a closed shop agreement. The NIRC, if it is not otherwise prevented from hearing the application, will send it to the CIR for investigation, and, on receiving their report, shall make an order allowing between one and three months for an application to be made by one-fifth of the workers who would be so covered by the agreement for a ballot. If no such application is made, the NIRC will confirm the approved closed shop agreement. If an application is made, the NIRC will request the CIR to arrange for a ballot to be held. If the requisite majority have voted in favour of the closed shop agreement the NIRC will make an order approving it; if such a majority is not obtained, the NIRC will not approve the proposals, and will not entertain any further such application in respect of those workers for two years.   [18]

Once an approved closed shop agreement has been established, then, after two years, an application may be made supported by one-fifth of the workers covered by the agreement for its discontinuance. Again, the ballot will be held, and if the requisite majority do not vote in favour of the continuance of the agreement, the NIRC will revoke its previous approval, the agreement will cease to be approved, and the matter cannot be raised again for two years in respect of those workers.   **[19]**

A closed shop agreement, of whatever nature, and however called, which has not been approved by the NIRC as above, is void.   **[20]**

(c) *Unfair dismissals* (see Chapter 7)

The Industrial Relations Act lays down important new principles relating to unfair dismissals. In some instances, however, satisfactory procedures for dealing with dismissals are already in existence. If so, all the parties to such a procedure agreement may apply for a designating order which will exclude the rights given under section 22 relating to unfair dismissals. The NIRC must be satisfied as to a number of things, in particular that the remedies provided for under the procedure agreement are no less beneficial than those provided by the Act (though they need not be the same). If it is so satisfied, an order will be made. Any of the parties, however, or the Secretary for State, may apply for the designating order to be revoked. If the NIRC is satisfied that all the parties wish to revoke the designating order, or if it thinks that the procedure agreement no longer fulfils the exempting provisions; the order will be revoked. The NIRC may make such transitional provisions as it deems appropriate.   **[21]**

(d) *Legally enforceable procedure agreements* (see Chapter 4)

If a procedure agreement is absent, or if it is defective, the Secretary of State, the employer, or a trade union, may make an application to the NIRC with a view to having a legally enforceable procedure agreement. The NIRC must be satisfied that the absence or defect has seriously impeded orderly industrial relations or that there has been substantial and repeated losses of working time, and if so it will refer the matter to the CIR, for their recommendations. The CIR may decide that it is necessary to enlarge the scope of the provisions, and may formulate new proposals. These will be transmitted to the NIRC and published. Anyone affected by the enlarged reference may apply to the NIRC, which may accept the enlarged reference, or direct that the original scope will remain unchanged. Failing such application, the NIRC will approve the extended reference. The CIR will investigate the reference (as extended, if necessary) with discussions among the parties with a view to obtaining their agreement on a new procedure agreement, so formulated as to be a legally enforceable contract. The reference may be withdrawn on an application to the NIRC if it is satisfied that the parties arrive at a satisfactory agreement for a legally enforceable contract. If not, the CIR must prepare their report with revised provisions. These will be sent to the NIRC and the parties to the reference. Within six months, any of the parties may apply to the NIRC, which unless it thinks that an order is not necessary for securing the observance and acceptance of the provisions, will make an order, defining the scope and the parties, and directing that after a specified date, the recommended provisions will take effect as a legally binding contract. Once a reference has been dealt with under the Act to the stage where the CIR makes their final report, the matter cannot be raised again before the NIRC for two years unless there are special circumstances. All the parties, however, may jointly apply for the revocation of the order of the NIRC, and even on the application of one of the parties, the NIRC will revoke the order if it thinks that it is no longer necessary (in this case, the CIR can be asked for an opinion).   [22]

(e) *Proposals for a sole bargaining agency* (see Chapter 4)

The provisions relating to sole bargaining agencies are designed to eliminate inter-union disputes over bargaining rights in a unit, and to ensure that employers concede bargaining rights in appropriate circumstances. A trade union may make an application that a particular group of employees shall be recognised as a bargaining unit, and that a particular trade union (or a joint negotiating panel if the application is made in respect of more than one union) shall be the bargaining agent. These questions may also be raised on an application to the NIRC by the Secretary of State or by an employer. [23]

The NIRC cannot entertain an application made by the parties unless they have notified the Secretary of State of the proposals, who may offer his assistance and advice. However, if the NIRC is satisfied that it is not precluded from hearing the application, and that the parties have attempted to settle the matter by negotiation or conciliation, and that a reference to the CIR is necessary to promote a lasting settlement, the problem will be sent to the CIR, specifying the questions to be determined by the Commission and the employer or employers and employees covered by the reference. The CIR may send the matter back to the NIRC at any time if they think that a satisfactory and lasting settlement has been reached, and the NIRC will withdraw the reference if it agrees with this recommendation. The CIR may also apply to the NIRC to extend the reference, and notice to interested parties must be given, but the extended reference will only be in respect of employees, not employers (other than an associated employer). Affected persons may apply to the NIRC, which will then extend the reference, limit it, or direct that the scope remains unchanged. The CIR will then prepare a report, and send copies to the NIRC, the Secretary of State, the employer(s), trade unions or other organisations of workers recommended for recognition as sole bargaining agent; the report may also be published in an appropriate manner. Within six months, the employer or the trade union(s) may apply to the NIRC, which will request the CIR to arrange for a ballot among the employees in question on the question whether the CIR's recommendations should be binding. The result of the ballot will be communicated to the NIRC, the employer and to the trade unions. If a simple majority of those voting in the ballot are in favour of the recommendations, the NIRC will make an order defining the bargaining unit, specifying the employer and trade union(s), and directing that after two months, and for as long as the order remains in force, that trade union shall be the sole bargaining agent for that bargaining unit.   [24]

Any employee affected by the sole bargaining agency may apply to the NIRC claiming that the organisation of workers recognised by the employer does not adequately represent the employees generally, or a particular section to which he belongs. If the NIRC has not yet made an order in relation to a sole bargaining agent, it will only hear this case if $\frac{1}{5}$ of the employees covered concur in the application. If a sole bargaining agency order has been made, the NIRC will not hear the application until after two years from the date of the order, and only on the application of $\frac{2}{5}$ of the employees covered. Subject to these provisos, the NIRC will ask the CIR to investigate and attempt to provide a settlement. If this fails, however, the NIRC shall ask the CIR to hold a ballot to determine the wishes of either all the employees or a particular section. The ballot will then be arranged. If all the employees are to be balloted, the question will be whether the trade union shall cease to be the bargaining agent. If a section of the employees is to be balloted, the question will be whether the trade union shall cease to be the bargaining agent for that section. The result of the ballot will be reported to the NIRC, the applicants, the employer and the trade union. If a simple majority of those voting are in favour of the proposal that the bargaining agency shall cease, the NIRC will then make an appropriate order, directing the employer not to treat that trade union as the bargaining agent for all employees or a section of his employees, as the case may be, and any previous order will be revoked or varied accordingly. A further application for sole bargaining agency recognition cannot be made in respect of those employees for two years.   [25]

Once an application for a sole bargaining agency is made to the

9

NIRC, the matter becomes a pending issue, and a strike, irregular industrial action, or a lock-out over that issue will become an unfair industrial practice, if called before the time when:

(a) the NIRC decides not to refer the matter to the CIR; or

(b) a reference to the CIR is withdrawn; or

(c) the expiration of six months from the date when the report of the CIR is sent to the NIRC.   [26]

(f) *Applications by and appeals from the Registrar* (see Chapter 2)

The Registrar of Trade Unions and Employers' Associations has important powers of control and supervision over the rules and activities of those bodies. Such powers, however, can only be exercised through the NIRC, and the Act makes the following provisions by way of appeals and applications.   [27]

(i) Cancellation of registration **(sections 76–77)**

The Registrar may apply to the NIRC for an order directing that the registration of a trade union or an employers' association shall be cancelled on the grounds that it has not submitted its rules or amended rules within the period allowed for this. The NIRC may either give the organisation concerned a further period within which it may alter and submit the rules, or, it can order the registration to be cancelled. If the trade union or employers' association has submitted the rules, but the Registrar has not approved them, then the organisation may apply to the NIRC either for an order allowing it a further period within which to amend those rules, or, an order directing the Registrar to approve the rules as submitted.   [28]

The Registrar may also apply to the NIRC for cancellation of registration where the registration was obtained by fraud or mistake, or where by reason of a change in the rules or other circumstances the organisation has ceased to be eligible for registration, or where the organisation has refused to comply with certain other requirements of the Industrial Relations Act after he has given it due notice of the default and given it not less than two months within which to rectify matters. In the latter case, the NIRC may extend the period of time within which the defect is to be corrected; in all cases, the NIRC can order the registration to be cancelled.   [29]

(ii) Individual complaints **(section 81)**

A person who complains of certain unfair industrial practices or of a breach of the rules by a trade union or employers' association may apply to the Registrar for an investigation. If the complaint is well founded, and a settlement has not been reached, and no complaint has been made to the industrial tribunal, and the Registrar thinks it is a serious breach, then he may present a case to the NIRC or the tribunal against the trade union or employers' association. The NIRC may make an order determining the rights of the original applicant, or award him compensation, or make an order calling on the organisation to refrain from such action.   [30]

(iii) Direct action by the Registrar (section 83)

If the Registrar suspects that there has been a breach of the rules, or the trade union or employers' association have acted contrary to the principles set out in section 65 or 69, as the case may be, and the organisation has not given an undertaking that it would desist from such action, or, having given the undertaking, it has not carried it out, then the Registrar may present a complaint to the NIRC. The NIRC will make an order directing the organisation to take such action as specified to mitigate the consequences, and to prevent further contravention of the rules or other conduct complained of.

[31]

(iv) Appeal from the Registrar's decision (section 115)

An appeal from the decision of the Registrar may be made

(a) against his rejection of an application for registration of a trade union or an employers' association;
(b) his refusal to place an organisation on the special register;
(c) his refusal to approve the rules, or any amended rules;
(d) in respect of the Registrar's decisions under sections 3 (2), 4 and 5 of the Trade Union Act 1913, relating to complaints of breaches of the rules of the political funds, and requiring the Registrar to approve the rules and to give certificates relating to the political funds;
(e) an appeal to the NIRC will also lie under section 4 (8) and (11) of the Trade Union (Amalgamations, etc.) Act 1964.   [32]

(g) *Complaints relating to unfair industrial practices* (section 101)

Any person may apply to the NIRC complaining that he has suffered from an unfair industrial practice which was taken against him or, in certain circumstances, which was taken against another person but which affects him. However, a complaint cannot be made in respect of a breach of section 5 (1) (rights in respect of trade union membership or non-membership) or section 22 (right not to be unfairly dismissed), for the remedies in these two cases must be pursued through the industrial tribunals (section 106). If the complaint is well founded, the NIRC may make an order determining the rights of the complainant or award compensation, or direct the offending party to desist from such action. If, however, the offender is an official acting within the scope of his authority on behalf of a trade union or employers' association, the NIRC cannot make either an award of compensation or a desisting order against the official,

11

but such remedies may be pursued against the organisation
concerned.   **[33]**

(h) *Complaints by trade unions* (see Chapter 5)

A trade union may present a complaint to the NIRC that an
employer:

(a) has failed to enter into an agency shop agreement despite the
result of a ballot being in favour of such; or

(b) that the employer is carrying on bargaining with an organisation of workers which was not recognised as such by a NIRC
order, or that the employer is not taking such action with a
view to carrying on bargaining as might be reasonably
expected to be taken as a result of a NIRC order conferring
bargaining rights (this is the nearest approach in the Act to the
American concept of "bargaining in good faith"); or

(c) that the employer has failed to disclose information without
which a union would be impeded in its bargaining activities,
and which ought to be disclosed in accordance with good
industrial relations practice.

In the case of (b) and (c) the NIRC can authorise the presentation
of a claim to the Industrial Arbitration Board. Additionally, in the
case of (a) and (c) the NIRC may make an order determining the
rights of the trade union, or an order directing the employer to take
such action as is necessary to fulfill the duty imposed on him. **[34]**

(i) *Receive applications from the Secretary of State* (see Chapter 6)

(i) Discontinuance of industrial action

If industrial action has begun or is threatened which, in the
opinion of the Secretary of State is likely to cause results which are
either gravely injurious to the national economy, or which may cause
serious risk of disease or personal injury to a substantial number of
persons, and he considers that the dispute may be solved by negotiation, conciliation or arbitration, he may apply to the NIRC for an
order to delay or postpone the industrial action for up to 60 days.
The application will specify the persons responsible, and they will
become parties to the application. If the NIRC thinks that there is
sufficient evidence for believing that there is a threat to the economic
interests of the country or that there is a risk to the health of sections
of the community, an order will be made accordingly. Henceforth, no
person named in the order may call or threaten any industrial action
in that area of employment, and any contrary orders may be counter-
manded. The order may be made for a period less than 60 days, but
the Secretary of State may apply to have that period extended, but
not so that the total period exceeds 60 days. After that period has

expired, the NIRC will not entertain any further application in respect of the same dispute.   [35]

(ii) Ordering a strike ballot

If the Secretary for State thinks that as a result of industrial action or a threat thereof there is a threat to the national economy, or risk of serious injury or disease to people, or the industrial action is likely to cause serious injury to the livelihoods of a substantial number of employees in the industry, and he thinks that there are reasons to doubt that there is a majority in favour of taking such strike action, he can apply to the NIRC for an order calling for a ballot on the issue. Before he does this, he is required to consult every employer or employers' association or trade union involved. The NIRC can then order a ballot, specifying the persons to be balloted, the question to be put, and the period within which the result of the ballot shall be reported back. Until then, no industrial action shall take place. The result of the ballot will be reported to the NIRC, which will publish it, and the order will lapse immediately. [36]

(j) *Miscellaneous powers and jurisdiction*

(i) Transfer of cases to and from the Industrial Tribunals **(section 111)**

The NIRC may direct that a case be transferred to it from an industrial tribunal, or, alternatively, the industrial tribunal may send a case to the NIRC to be heard there. In the latter instance, the NIRC may hear it, or send it back to the Industrial Tribunal as being a more suitable forum. If the NIRC hears the case, it will have all the jurisdiction the tribunal would have had, and has power to apply the same remedies.   [37]

(ii) Appeals from the industrial tribunals to the NIRC **(section 114)**

The Lord Chancellor may, by statutory instrument, provide that an appeal will lie to the NIRC on a point of law arising from any case being dealt with by the Industrial Tribunal under any of the following:

(a) the Contracts of Employments Act 1963;
(b) the Redundancy Payments Act 1965;
(c) the Equal Pay Act 1970;
(d) a complaint under the Industrial Relations Act; or
(e) any matter arising out of the jurisdiction conferred on the Industrial Tribunals by section 113 of the Industrial Relations Act (in relating to claims for damages for breach of any contract of employment).

It would seem, therefore, that if the issue involves a question of fact, an appeal lies to the ordinary courts in the usual way.   [38]

13

(iii) Compensation awards **(sections 116, 117, 118)**

On any complaint before the NIRC or an industrial tribunal the court or tribunal may award such compensation as it thinks to be just and equitable, having regard to the loss suffered. This will include any expense incurred, and the loss of any benefit which might reasonably have been expected. The complainant is, however, subject to the common law duty to mitigate against his loss as far as possible. Compensation may be reduced if the complainant contributed to the cause of the loss. If a complaint refers to an unfair dismissal, and the Industrial Tribunal has recommended re-engagement which the applicant has unreasonably refused, the compensation shall be reduced. If, however, the employer has failed to comply with the recommendation for re-engagement, the award may be increased, to such an extent as the court or tribunal considers to be just and equitable. Appropriate limits are placed on the amount of compensation which can be awarded in favour of an individual, and against a trade union.   **[39]**

(iv) Proceedings in contract **(sections 129, 130)**

(a) Only the NIRC has jurisdiction to hear cases relating to the construction or effect of collective agreements or applications to enforce or obtain damages or compensation for breach of a collective agreement.

(b) Actions in the High Court or county court relating to a breach of a contract of employment in respect of which an action is pending before the industrial tribunal or the NIRC may be stayed as appropriate.   **[40]**

(v) Proceedings in tort **(section 131)**

The purpose of the Industrial Relations Act is to confine the majority of potential actions relating to industrial relations questions to the NIRC or the industrial tribunals. Accordingly, if any proceedings in tort are brought in any other court, the action may be stayed if the court considers that either the act is the subject of proceedings before the NIRC or industrial tribunal, or is one in respect of which (as being an unfair industrial practice or breach of duty) proceedings ought rightfully to be brought before the NIRC or tribunal. Conversely, the NIRC has no jurisdiction other than that conferred by the Industrial Relations Act, and thus is itself precluded from hearing other tort actions.   **[41]**

(vi) An employee may present a complaint to the NIRC that his employer has failed to comply with an order from the Industrial Tribunal requiring the employer to issue him with an annual statement.   **[42]**

(vii) Review of ballots **(section 160)**

If, as a result of any ballot taken by or under the supervision of the CIR for the purpose of establishing or discontinuing agency shops, approved closed shops, or sole bargaining agencies, the NIRC finds that the report made by the CIR was incorrect, and that it would be just and equitable to rectify the error without requiring a further ballot to be taken, the court may make an order amending the report, which will then have effect as amended. If, on the other hand, the NIRC finds that the ballot was misconducted so that it would not be just and equitable to regard it as valid, or that the report of the CIR could not be corrected as above, the NIRC will make an order quashing the ballot and so much of the report of the CIR as relates to that ballot. If the NIRC has already made an order as a result of the defective ballot, the order will be revoked. If the NIRC does quash the ballot, the resulting situation will be as if the ballot had not been taken. The rules of the NIRC will provide as to the circumstances in which, and by whom, an application may be made for such review, the circumstances in which the NIRC may so act without such an application, and the persons who may be made parties to any proceedings in which the NIRC is considering making such an order. The NIRC has no such power in respect of a ballot held under section 142 (ballot in situations of national emergencies, see Chapter 6), for such a ballot is designed to test the strength of feelings of the workers involved, and it does not confer any binding legal obligation.   **[42A]**

B. THE SECRETARY OF STATE FOR THE DEPARTMENT OF EMPLOYMENT

The Secretary of State has a number of initiating functions under the Industrial Relations Act. He is, of course, the Minister primarily responsible for the state of industrial relations, and as such may be expected to play an important role under the new law. The broad headings of his responsibilities are as follows: **[43]**

(a) *Code of Industrial Relations Practice* **(section 2)**

His first task under the Act, which must be carried out before the end of a year, is to lay before Parliament a new Code of Industrial Relations Practice, which will contain such practical guidance as he thinks would be helpful for the purpose of enabling the parties to conform to the four principles set out at the beginning of this chapter. The code may be revised from time to time after consultation with the T.U.C. and the C.B.I. and taking into account any advice he may receive on the subject from the CIR. The Code will pay particular regard to the need for employers to ·disclose information for bargaining purposes, though they will not be required to disclose confidential information, or information which is secret or information the disclosure of which may otherwise seriously affect the interests of the employer or the interests of national security (section 158 (2)). The Code will also pay attention to the establishment and maintenance of effective means of information and communication at all levels between workers and the management.   **[44]**

The Code will be laid before Parliament, and is to be approved by a resolution of both Houses. The Secretary of State will specify the date on which it is to be brought into effect. A failure on the part of any person to observe the Code will not itself render that person liable to any proceedings, but in any case coming before the NIRC or an industrial tribunal the Code will be admissible in evidence and any relevant provision will be taken into account so far as that case is concerned (section 4).   **[45]**

(b) *Powers in relation to unfair dismissals* (see Chapter 7)
If an exemption to the unfair dismissals provisions has been obtained the Secretary of State may apply to the NIRC for that exemption to be revoked. He will do this if he considers that the procedure agreement in question has ceased to fulfil all the exempting conditions.
        [46]

(c) *Powers in relation to collective bargaining* (see Chapter 4)
If a procedural agreement is absent or unsuitable in a particular undertaking, or if the one which is in existence is constantly being broken, the Secretary of State may apply to the NIRC, which will then set in motion machinery which may lead to a legally enforceable agreement being drawn up.   **[47]**

He may also apply to the NIRC in respect of an application for a sole bargaining agency though he must first consult with any employer or organisation of workers appearing to him to be directly concerned in the application. He will request that the CIR should examine questions relating to the definition of a bargaining unit, and whether an organisation of workers or joint negotiating panel should act as the sole bargaining agency. If an employer or a trade union makes an application for a sole bargaining agency, the Secretary of State must first be notified of the proposals, and he shall give such advice and assistance as he may consider to be appropriate with a view to promoting an agreement, and, for this purpose, he may refer any question to the CIR for examination.   **[48]**

(d) *Notification of procedures agreements* (see Chapter 4)
The Secretary of State may make regulations requiring certain employers to inform him if they are party to any procedure agreement, to furnish him with a copy of it, or, in the case of an employer

who is not a party to an agreement but who has otherwise agreed to abide by one, to send a copy or furnish him with sufficient particulars as to enable him to identify it. The employer will also be required to inform the Secretary of State of the descriptions of the different categories of employees who fall within each procedure agreement.
[49]

(e) *References to the CIR* (section 121)

The Secretary of State acting alone or jointly with other Ministers may refer to the CIR any question relating to industrial relations generally, or in respect of any particular industry. In particular he may refer a number of specified subjects, including:

(a) the manner in which employers or workers are organised for the purpose of collective bargaining, including questions of amalgamation or co-operation between the various bodies concerned;
(b) procedure agreements, or the need for them where they do not exist;
(c) any matter for which a procedure agreement can provide;
(d) recognition and negotiating rights;
(e) disclosure of information to employees or trade union representatives who have negotiating rights;
(f) facilities for training people in industrial relations or collective bargaining.   [50]

(f) *Emergency procedures* (see Chapter 6)

(i) Subject to certain conditions the Secretary of State may apply to the NIRC for an order postponing a strike or irregular industrial action or a lock-out for a period up to 60 days.   [52]

(ii) Subject to certain conditions he may apply to the NIRC for an order requiring a ballot to be taken among those who may go on strike or use other irregular industrial action, to ascertain their wishes in this respect.   [53]

(g) *Appointment of Conciliation Officers* (section 146)

The Secretary of State may appoint a number of conciliation officers who will continue to perform their traditional functions dating from the Conciliation Act 1896 in addition to those conferred on them by the Industrial Relations Act.   [54]

(i) On a complaint to the Industrial Tribunal relating to any matter contained in section 5 (1) (right of a person to belong, or not to belong to a trade union) or section 22 (right not to be unfairly dismissed) a copy of the complaint, together with the employer's reply, must be sent to the conciliation officer. The parties must be notified that the services of the conciliation officer are available to

17

them, and the proceedings before the tribunal may be postponed for a period to enable the processes of conciliation to be given a chance to settle the dispute.   [55]

The conciliation officer will attempt to promote a settlement if the employer and employee request him to do so, or if he thinks he could attempt this with a reasonable prospect of success. If the employee in question has been dismissed, a conciliation officer will attempt to obtain his re-engagement, failing which he will try, with his consent, to obtain an agreement on the amount of compensation to be payable.   [56]

(ii) He will also make his services available on request in respect of the two matters mentioned (sections 5 (1) and 22 cases) even though no claim for compensation has been presented to the industrial tribunal. He may also perform services (by direction of the Secretary of State) in matters where a claim is made for damages for breach of contract of employment under the provisions of section 113.
                                                                      [57]

(iii) The rules of the NIRC will provide that the court shall so exercise its jurisdiction so as to enable the parties to avail themselves of the services of conciliation officers or other opportunities for conciliation. Anything communicated to the conciliation officer in connection with the performance of his functions shall not be admissible in evidence before the NIRC or the Industrial Tribunal without the consent of the person making the communication. [58]

(h) *Miscellaneous powers*

(i) By the Race Relations Act 1968 the Secretary of State has certain powers in respect of acts of racial discrimination. Those powers are not to be exercised under that Act if the case would be suitable for bringing before the Industrial Tribunal under the Industrial Relations Act, though if there is an unfair industrial practice (whether relating to a dismissal or otherwise), the Secretary of State may seek a written assurance that the action will not be repeated, and may bring proceedings under the Race Relations Act if that assurance has been broken.   [59]

(ii) The Secretary of State is empowered to make the following additional regulations and orders:

(a) in respect of a possible overlapping which may occur if a person is unfairly dismissed and at the same time has received or is claiming redundancy payment;

(b) to provide for the continuity of employment for the purposes of the Redundancy Payments Act where a person is unfairly dismissed;

(c) shortening the period of time within which a worker must make his payments when an agency shop or an approved closed shop agreement has been reached;

(d) with respect to the inspection of the registers and other documents kept by the Registrar and the fees to be charged for such inspection;

(e) applying the term "worker" to a person who is the holder of an office;

(f) limiting applications made to the NIRC in respect of;

   (i) agency shop agreements
   (ii) enforceable procedural agreements
   (iii) sole bargaining agencies
   (iv) failure to disclose information to trade union officials unless the number of persons employed in the undertaking exceed a specified number;

(g) increase or decrease the number of members of the CIR;

(h) in respect of proceedings before the industrial tribunals;

(i) in respect of the information which must be disclosed to employees in major undertakings.

(j) add to, or vary, or exclude, the provisions of sections 27 and 28 (cases excluded from the unfair dismissals provisions);

(k) conferring exemptions on the duty of undertakings to disclose information;

(l) requiring firms which employ more or fewer than 350 employees to disclose information to their employees;

(m) increase the limit of compensation payable to individuals to a sum greater than £4,160 in total;

(n) calculating the amount of a week's pay for compensation purposes;

(o) to enable members of trade unions to nominate persons entitled to receive certain death benefits;

(p) bringing the Act into operation;

(q) making transitional provisions;

(r) where the Lord Chancellor is empowered to make certain orders relating to conferring jurisdiction on the industrial tribunals in respect of damages for breach of contracts of employment (section 113), or appeals from the tribunals to the NIRC, the Secretary of State has similar powers relating to Scotland.   **[60]**

(iii) Every claim made by a trade union or employers' association to the Industrial Arbitration Board under the section 8 of the Terms and Conditions of Employment Act 1959 must be reported to the Secretary of State.   **[61]**

C. THE COMMISSION ON INDUSTRIAL RELATIONS

The Donovan Commission recommended that a permanent Commission on Industrial Relations should be set up, with certain functions. The Government of the day accepted that recommendation at once, and the Commission came into existence in 1969 by virtue of a Royal Warrant. The Act, therefore, merely confirms the CIR on a statutory basis, but at the same time, has increased vastly its role and functions under the new organisational structure. **[62]**

The CIR will consist of between six and fifteen members, who are appointed by the Secretary of State. A member may serve for five years, and is eligible for re-appointment after that time. The Secretary of State may remove a member of the Commission on the grounds of incapacity or misbehaviour. The CIR have their own staff. They are empowered to secure certain information (such as the names and addresses of employees who are to be balloted) are given general powers in relation to the holding of enquiries, and will act as a commission of enquiry under the Wages Council Act 1959. They may invite employers to provide premises and other facilities for enabling any ballot to be taken. **[63]**

The Secretary of State will refer certain general matters to the CIR. After examining the question, the CIR will report back to the Minister, and the report may be published if it is thought expedient to do so. If, however, a matter so referred becomes the subject of a reference to the CIR by the NIRC, then the latter reference shall be proceeded with in accordance with the provisions of the Act, and the reference by the Secretary of State shall not be proceeded with further. The CIR must produce an annual report on their activities, which will include a general review of the development of collective bargaining, drawing attention to any particular problems. In respect of these general matters, the work of the CIR extends to N. Ireland. **[64]**

The following specific functions are carried out by the CIR on instructions from the NIRC. **[65]**

(a) *Agency shop applications* (see Chapter 4)

Before taking a ballot on this question, if the CIR consider that the matter of sole negotiating rights ought first to be settled, they shall report this to the NIRC, and will not proceed with the ballot. Apart from this, they will decide if the ballot should extend to all the workers specified in the application, or some of them, or additional persons not specified in the application, and shall report on this to the NIRC. The CIR will also decide whether to conduct the ballot themselves, or whether this should be conducted under the supervision of another body, and to make arrangements in either case to

20

ensure a properly conducted secret ballot. The result of the ballot will be reported to the NIRC, to the employer, trade union or negotiating panel as the case may be. The CIR has similar functions if the question raised is the discontinuance of the agency shop. **[66]**

(b) *Approved closed shop agreements* (see Chapter 4)

On receipt from the NIRC of a reference to examine an approved closed shop agreement, the CIR will consider if such an agreement is absolutely necessary, and will report their conclusions to the NIRC and the applicants. They will arrange a ballot if so requested, making the usual arrangements, and report the result to the NIRC and the parties. A similar ballot will be so organised if there is an application for the discontinuance of an approved closed shop agreement.   **[67]**

(c) *Absence of procedures* (see Chapter 4)

The NIRC will refer to the CIR the questions as to whether in a particular undertaking the procedure is either absent or defective, and their recommendations will be sought. If the CIR think that the defects do exist, and that the remedy lies in bringing new provisions into effect or the revision of existing provisions, or new provisions ought to apply to a larger unit, they will after consulting the employer and any affected trade union, formulate proposals accordingly. These will be sent to the NIRC, and to the affected parties. The CIR may also recommend that other parties shall be added to the reference, and having clarified the reference and the parties, shall seek their agreement to a new or improved procedure, capable of having effect as a legally binding contract. At any time the CIR may decide that the purpose for which the reference was made has been adequately fulfilled without continuing in the matter further, and shall report to this effect to the NIRC, which may, on the application of any of the parties, withdraw the reference.   **[68]**

(d) *Sole bargaining agency* (see Chapter 4)

If the NIRC is satisfied that the relevant conditions are fulfilled, it will refer to the CIR an application for a sole bargaining agency. The CIR may at any time ask the NIRC to withdraw the reference on the grounds that the parties have come to a satisfactory and lasting settlement. The CIR may also formulate proposals for extending the reference, which will be transmitted to the NIRC and to person affected thereby. The latter may apply to the NIRC to consider whether such proposals are in fact necessary or expedient, and the NIRC will extend the reference as suggested, or modify it, or direct that the original reference be unchanged. The CIR will then prepare a report setting out their recommendations, which will be sent to the Secretary of State, the employer and the trade unions affected, and published as appropriate.   [69]

For the purpose of determining the composition of the bargaining unit, the CIR will consider the extent to which different employees in a particular group have interests in common, having regard to the nature of their work, and their training, experience, professional or other qualifications. An organisation of workers will not be recommended for recognition as the sole bargaining agent unless it appears to the CIR that it is independent (e.g., it is not a "house" union), and its recognition as such would be in accordance with the general wishes of the employees comprised in that unit, and would promote a satisfactory and lasting settlement to the question in issue.   [70]

In determining this, they will take into account whether or not the bargaining agent has sufficient resources to effectively represent those employees, and whether the bargaining agent would have the support of a substantial number of the employees in the bargaining unit. The CIR may also recommend the like formation of a joint negotiating bargaining panel, comprising of more than one organisation of workers. They may require the bargaining agent to make available a sufficient number of trained officials for the purpose of collective bargaining, or may restrict the right of the bargaining agent to act as such in respect of other employees. If there are already in existence more extensive bargaining arrangements (e.g., a national agreement), the CIR may specify them in their recommendations, and the bargaining agency may be subject to the reservation that the bargaining agent may not have exclusive negotiating rights in respect of the matters dealt with by those specified arrangements. The CIR shall, if directed to do so by the NIRC, arrange for a ballot to be conducted, allowing for a reasonable interval of time after the publication of its report, in order to allow interested parties to consider its implications.   [71]

In respect of an application for the discontinuance of a sole bargaining agency made to the NIRC, the CIR shall endeavour to promote discussions which might lead to a settlement, but if this fails, the NIRC will again request CIR to arrange for a ballot to be held, the result of which will be reported to the NIRC, the employer, the applicant and the affected trade unions.   [72]

(e) *Functions in relation to the emergency powers procedure* (see Chapter 6)

The CIR has no role to play in respect of an application by the Secretary of State for a 60 day "cooling off" order, but if an application has been made by the Secretary of State for a ballot on strike or irregular industrial action the NIRC may invite the CIR to assist in formulating any order relating to the area of employment in respect of which the ballot is to be taken, and the question to be put on the ballot. The CIR may request a trade union to conduct the ballot under its supervision, for which reasonable expenses will be paid. Otherwise, the CIR will conduct it or arrange for some other body to conduct it, and, in either case, the CIR will ensure that the ballot is properly conducted and that voting in the ballot is kept secret. The result will be notified to the NIRC.   [73]

D. THE REGISTRAR OF THE TRADE UNIONS AND EMPLOYERS' ASSOCIATIONS

The Act creates the new office of Chief Registrar of Trade Unions and Employers' Associations, and assistant registrars may be appointed. A report of the activities of the registrars will be laid before Parliament every year.   [74]

The Registrar has wide powers of administrative control over trade unions and employers' associations; he can investigate complaints, and, in the last resort, may present complaints to the NIRC or the industrial tribunals. His main functions may be outlined as follows: [75]

(a) *Keeping a provisional register* (see Chapter 2)

The first duty of the Registrar, when appointed, will be to draw up a provisional register, which will be kept until all the entries therein are cancelled. Every trade union and employers' association which immediately before the passing of the Industrial Relations Act is registered under the Trade Union Acts of 1871–1964 will be put on the provisional register, and any organisation which applies within six months from the passing of the Act (on the grounds that although it is not registered under the 1871–1964 Acts, it is a trade union within the meaning of those Acts) shall also be placed on the provisional register. The registrar will then consider each entry on the provisional register, to see if the organisation is eligible for registration under the Act. If, within six months from the date of the entry in the provisional register, he is so satisfied, he will cancel that entry and issue a certificate of registration. If he is not so satisfied, he will serve a notice of that fact on the organisation. The organisation will then have six months (or such further period as the Registrar may allow) to take any necessary steps to alter its rules in order to be eligible for registration, after which time, unless the organisation makes a fresh application, the entry in the provisional register will be cancelled. If a fresh application is made, the Registrar will either cancel the provisional entry and register the organisation under the Industrial Relations Act, or, if he still rejects the application, will cancel the provisional entry as soon as the time for making an appeal to the NIRC has expired without an appeal being made, or, if it has been made, if his decision is upheld by the NIRC. The Registrar will also cancel the entry in the provisional register if the organisation requests him to do so, or if he is satisfied that it no longer exists.   **[76]**

The effect of the entry on the provisional register is important. A body so entered will be entitled, temporarily at least, to the protections which a registered trade union or employers' association will have under the Act, namely, under section 96 (immunity from an action based on inducing a breach of contract), section 117 (limitation on the amount of compensation to be awarded against trade unions) and section 153 (recovery of sums awarded against trade unions and employers' associations). Also, the right to join a trade union (as laid down in section 5 (1)) applies to those organisations of workers on the provisional register and a member of such organisation may nominate persons entitled to receive certain death benefits from a trade union. These apart, entry on the provisional register does not constitute registration for the purposes of the Act.
                                                                        [77]

(b) *Register of trade unions and employers' associations* (see Chapter 2)

An independent organisation of workers, or an organisation of employers, may apply for registration under the Act, and as long as the formalities have been complied with the Registrar must issue a certificate of registration. An appeal against the refusal of registration may be made to the NIRC. As soon after the issue of a certificate as is practical the Registrar will examine the rules of the organisation, and if they are defective in accordance with certain principles he will serve a notice on the organisation, indicating what alterations are necessary for the purpose of remedying the defect. He will give a reasonable period for the organisation to alter and re-submit the rules, and if they are still not satisfactory he can reject them once more, again allowing a reasonable period for alteration and re-submission. If the rules are still defective, the Registrar will apply to the NIRC for the registration to be cancelled. The Registrar may also apply to the NIRC for cancellation of registration if this was obtained by fraud or mistake, or if the organisation has so changed its rules so as to be ineligible for registration, or the organisation has failed to comply with certain other requirements of the Act, despite a notice from the Registrar specifying the default and calling for this to be remedied.   **[78]**

(c) *Special register* (see Chapter 3)

There are a number of organisations which, although not trade unions in the normal sense, do play a role in the collective bargaining process on behalf of their members. To bring such bodies within the scope of the Act (mainly for bargaining purposes) the Registrar will keep a special register. An appeal against the refusal of the Registrar to put the organisation concerned in the special register may be made to the NIRC.   [79]

(d) *Investigatory powers* (see Chapter 2)

A person who is or was a member of a trade union or employers' association, or who has been prevented from obtaining, or has been refused, membership, may apply to the Registrar alleging that the organisation has committed an unfair industrial practice against him, or that there has been a breach of the rules. If the organisation has an adequate procedure for dealing with complaints, and the applicant has not used it, the Registrar shall defer consideration of the complaint. He may resume consideration if it is re-submitted after the procedure has been invoked.

The Registrar, if he is satisfied that the application is within the provisions of the Act, and is not frivolous or vexatious, may investigate the complaint, and give notice of his conclusions to the applicant and the organisation. If the complaint is well founded, he will endeavour to promote a settlement, and any communication made to him in his endeavours shall not be admissible before the NIRC or the Industrial Tribunal without the consent of the person who made it. If no settlement is reached, and the applicant does not present a case to the Tribunal, but the Registrar considers that the matter is a serious one, he may present a case either to the NIRC or to an industrial tribunal.   [80]

The Registrar may also initiate investigations on his own behalf. He will do this if he becomes aware that there has been a serious breach or persistent breaches of the organisation's rules (except in two specified cases) or there is a serious breach of the guiding principles for such organisations which are set down in the Act. He will then serve a notice calling for such action as is necessary to remedy or mitigate the consequences and to prevent a continuance of the breach or action in question. If the organisation fails or refuses to give the required undertaking, the Registrar may give notice that unless the organisation takes the required action or gives a specified undertaking within a certain period, he intends to refer the whole matter to the NIRC.   [81]

(e) *Administrative control over registered organisations* (see Chapter 2)

Every trade union and employers' association must keep proper accounts, a register of members, and must send to the Registrar an annual return. In addition, he must be notified within one month of every change in the rules, or change of officers, or change of the address of its principal office. **[82]**

If the Registrar believes that an organisation is insolvent, he may appoint an inspector to examine its affairs. If the inspector confirms this belief, the Registrar may apply to the *High Court* for the organisation to be wound up by the court in accordance with the Companies Act 1948, as an unregistered company. **[83]**

E. INDUSTRIAL TRIBUNALS

These tribunals were set up in 1964, and have existing jurisdiction over matters arising from:

(a) Industrial Training Act 1964;
(b) the Contracts of Employment Act 1963;
(c) the Redundancy Payments Act 1965;
(d) the Docks and Harbours Act 1966;
(e) the Selective Employment Payments Act 1966;
(f) the Equal Pay Act 1970.

To this jurisdiction a number of matters are added by the Industrial Relations Act. **[84]**

The tribunals sit in regional centres, and it is likely that additional tribunals will be created for the purposes of the Act. A tribunal consists of a legally qualified chairman, with two other members. The procedure is informal, and the parties may be represented by a lawyer, or trade union official, or any other person of their choosing. Any award made by way of compensation may be enforced by execution issued from a county court, i.e., by distraint or attachment of earnings[4]. If a case is brought before the tribunal in respect of sections 5 (1) or 22 a copy must be sent to the conciliation officer, and the complainant and the employer against whom it is made must be notified that the services of the conciliation officer are available and the case may be postponed temporarily to enable the conciliation processes to be given an opportunity to settle the dispute amicably. The tribunals will determine cases in accordance with "just and equitable" principles in the same manner as the NIRC, and the principles of the limits of the amount of compensation to be payable are the same before the Industrial Tribunals as they are before the NIRC. The tribunal may sit in private to hear evidence

---

[4] In Scotland, as a recorded decree arbital.

which may be against the interests of national security to allow it to be given in public, or which is of a confidential nature. A complaint in respect of an unfair dismissal must be presented within four weeks of the effective date of the termination of the employment, while a complaint relating to a breach of section 5 must be presented within four weeks of the date of the action complained of. The tribunal, however, can hear the case even though it was not presented within the specified time if it is satisfied that it was not practicable for the complaint to be presented earlier (e.g., if the applicant was ill, etc.). Complaints brought in respect of an unfair industrial practice under section 66 or a breach of the rules must be brought within four weeks from the date when the action complained of was committed, or when it came to the notice of the applicant, or, if the Registrar has investigated the matter under section 81, the date when he gave notice of his conclusions or notice of his intention not to proceed with the matter further.   **[85]**

The following matters may be brought before the Industrial Tribunals:

(a) *Contribution to a trade union* (see Chapter 4)

If an agency shop has been established an individual who is not a member of a trade union may be required to make a contribution to the union. If he alleges that the contribution demanded is not payable in accordance with the agreement, or is in excess of the limit provided by the Act, he can apply to have the dispute determined by the tribunal. If he objects on conscientious grounds to paying to the union, the tribunal may be asked to decide if his objections are genuine. The question of which charity shall receive the contribution, and how much is payable may likewise be determined in the event of a dispute. Similar matters, with appropriate modifications, may be brought before the industrial tribunal in respect of an approved closed shop agreement.   **[86]**

(b) *Complaints against an employer* (see Chapter 7)

A complaint against an employer may be brought on the ground that the employer has violated the worker's right under section 5 (right to belong or not to belong to a trade union) or section 22 (unfair dismissal). The complaint must normally be brought within four weeks of the act complained of if it is in respect of an unfair dismissal. In respect of a section 5 application, the tribunal may

(a) make an order determining the rights of the applicant, and/or
(b) award compensation to the applicant against the employer.

Where the complaint is made under section 22, the tribunal may make a *recommendation* that the applicant be re-engaged by the employer or his successor or by an associated employer on terms that it thinks reasonable. If this recommendation is not made, or if it is not complied with for whatever reasons, an award of compensation can be made against the employer in favour of the applicant.   **[87]**

A complaint may also be made on the ground that the employer has failed to provide the claimant with an annual statement. The tribunal can declare the claimant's rights, and order the employer to provide such statement within a specified time.   **[88]**

The Lord Chancellor may, by statutory instrument, provide that the tribunals may hear any action for damages in respect of any breach of a contract of employment (by either party) other than damages for personal injuries; damages are the only remedy under this provision.   **[89]**

(c) *Complaints against organisations* (see Chapter 2)

Any person who is or was a member of an organisation of workers or an organisation of employers, and who did not resign voluntarily, or any person who has sought and been refused admission or been prevented from obtaining admission, may bring an action in respect of an unfair industrial practice in accordance with the provisions of section 66 or 70, or in respect of a breach of the rules of the organisation. The tribunal will not hear the case if an application for an investigation by the Registrar has been made and the Registrar has not concluded his investigations. If the tribunal finds that the complaint is justified, it can award the following remedies;

(a) an order determining the rights of the complainant;
(b) compensation to be paid by the organisation.

If a complaint has been made to the Registrar under section 81 which has been investigated, but no settlement has been reached, and the Registrar does not propose to refer the matter to the NIRC, and the original complainant has not referred the matter to the tribunal, the Registrar may do so on his own initiative. If the complaint is in respect of an unfair industrial practice under section 66 or 70, or is a breach of the rules of the organisation the tribunal will grant like remedies as if the complainant had brought the case.   **[90]**

(d) *Appeals to the NIRC*

The Lord Chancellor may by statutory instrument provide that appeals on point of law from the decisions of the tribunals (other than matters arising from the Selective Employment Payments Act and the Docks and Harbours Act) will be made to the NIRC in all cases. Appeals on questions of fact will therefore still be heard as at present, by the ordinary courts.   **[91]**

F. INDUSTRIAL ARBITRATION BOARD

The Industrial Court, which has been in existence since 1919, is to be renamed the Industrial Arbitration Board. It consists of a President (appointed by the Minister) and normally has two other members, representing both sides of industry. It will continue to exercise its former functions of arbitration (with mutual consent) and can give advice on any matter referred to it by the Minister within the limits laid down in the Industrial Courts Act 1919. The IAB will also continue its work in respect of the Fair Wages clauses, and under the Terms and Conditions of Employment Act 1959. The following additional points should be noted: **[92]**

(a) *Refusal to recognise a sole bargaining agent, or failure to bargain* (see Chapter 4)

If a trade union alleges that the employer has been guilty of an unfair industrial practice in that the employer has not taken such action with regard to bargaining with that agent as might reasonably be expected, the NIRC may order the presentation of a claim to the IAB. The claim will specify the employees in respect of whom it is being brought, and will ask that with regard to them the employer shall observe certain specified terms and conditions of employment. The claim may only be brought on behalf of those employees who were the subject of an order from the NIRC. The IAB will make an award that the employer shall observe the terms and conditions of employment which are claimed, or such other terms and conditions which it considers to be more appropriate, which will become an implied term of the contract of employment of those workers. The award may be made retrospective but cannot be dated earlier than the time when the NIRC found that the unfair industrial practice occurred.   **[93]**

(b) *Failure to disclose information for bargaining purposes* (see Chapter 4)

An employer is under a duty to disclose to trade union representatives such information without which a trade union would be impeded in its bargaining, and which in accordance with good industrial relations practice ought to be disclosed. The Code of Industrial Relations Practice will lay down guidelines on this, but it is not to be conclusive. If a trade union considers the employer is failing in this duty, it should apply to the NIRC, which, in addition to the power to make an order on the rights of the trade union, and directing the employer to take such action as is necessary to fulfil

29

its duty, may also order that a claim be presented to the IAB. The IAB will make the award as above, but it cannot be backdated earlier than the time when the NIRC decided that the employer was in breach of his duty.   **[94]**

CHAPTER TWO

TRADE UNIONS

The Act defines an "organisation of workers" as an organisation, whether permanent or temporary, which either:

(a) consists wholly or mainly or workers of one of more description and is an organisation whose principle objects include the regulation of relations between those workers and employers or organisations of employers; or

(b) is a federation of workers' organisations.   [95]

The term "worker" means any person who works, or seeks to work under a contract of employment, or any other contract whereby he undertakes to perform personally work or services (other than in a professional capacity) or is employed by a government department other than as a member of the Armed Forces. The term also includes certain persons employed under the National Health Service. [96]

A federation of workers means an organisation (temporary or permanent) which consist of organisations (or representatives of such organisations) each of which fulfil the conditions in (a) above, and whose principle objects include the regulation of relations between workers and employers or organisations of employers, or include the regulation of relations between its affiliated or constituent organisations.[1]   [97]

An organisation which is registered in the special register under the Act (see page 57, below) may also be included within the meaning of the terms "organisation of workers" or "federations of workers' organisations" for certain purposes.   [98]

A trade union, on the other hand, is defined simply as an organisation of workers which is registered as a trade union under the Act.
               [99]

[1] E.g., the T.U.C.

31

The result, therefore, is that there are six types of organisations which come within the scope of the Act, as follows:

ORGANISATION OF WORKERS

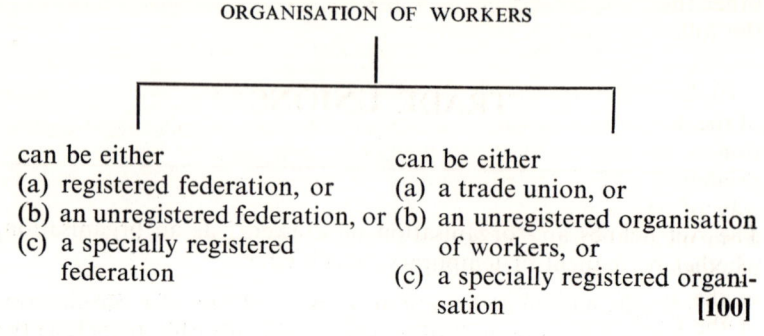

can be either	can be either
(a) registered federation, or	(a) a trade union, or
(b) an unregistered federation, or	(b) an unregistered organisation of workers, or
(c) a specially registered federation	(c) a specially registered organisation [100]

Great care must be taken with the use of these respective terms, for not all of the provisions of the Act cover all the organisations concerned. In particular, we must distinguish between registered organisations, unregistered organisations, and specially registered organisations. It is vital to know in any particular case the legal status of the organisation concerned, for, in general, only those which are registered under the Act are entitled to benefit from the privileges and immunities conferred. Hitherto, registration has been an unimportant matter; in future, it is likely to be crucial. In other respects, all organisations of workers, whether registered or not, will be subject to a varying degree of control, and will be expected to conform to the specified standards. In this chapter, we are mainly concerned with trade unions and registered federations of trade unions, though many of the provisions discussed will be applicable to other organisations. [101]

The Act provides (section 135) that the purpose of any trade union or other organisation of workers or any voluntary joint negotiating body shall not, by reason only that they are in restraint of trade, be unlawful so as

(a) to make any members of the organisation liable to criminal proceedings for conspiracy or otherwise; or
(b) to make any agreement or trust void or voidable.

This provision is a re-enactment of similar provisions in the Trade Union Act 1871, and is necessary in order to avoid the re-occurrence of certain common law rules which could inhibit trade union activity by virtue of the doctrine of criminal conspiracy. The matter basically is of historical importance only. [102]

A. GUIDING PRINCIPLES (section 65)

Every organisation of workers, whether a trade union or not, other than a federation of workers' organisations, shall conform to the following general principles.

(i) Every person who applies for membership and who is a worker of the description of which in accordance with the rules the organisation is intended wholly or mainly to consist, and who is appropriately qualified for employment in that description, shall not, by way of any arbitrary or unreasonable discrimination, be excluded from membership. This principle follows the reasoning in the case of *Nagle* v. *Fielden*[2] where the plaintiff, who was a woman, applied to the Jockey Club for a trainer's licence. It was unwritten policy of the Club not to grant licences to women, and the plaintiff sued for a declaration that this unwritten rule was contrary to public policy. It was held that at common law, a person had a right to pursue his or her trade or profession without being arbitrarily excluded therefrom. So far as workers' organisations are concerned, therefore, the rule has statutory backing.

(ii) Every person has the right, on giving reasonable notice, and complying with any reasonable conditions, to resign as a member at any time.

(iii) No member shall, by way of any arbitrary or unreasonable discrimination be excluded from:

(a) being a candidate for, or holding any office;
(c) nominating candidates for such office;
(c) voting in any election for any such office or in any ballot of members;
(d) attending and taking part in any meetings of the organisation.

The effect of this principle is that, for example, the rules of some trade unions, which debar communists or fascists from holding office, will now require alteration.

(iv) The voting in any ballot of members shall be secret.

(v) In any ballot, and on any motion, in respect of which a member is entitled to vote, he shall have a fair and reasonable opportunity to do so without interference or constraint.

(vi) No member shall be subject to unfair or unreasonable disciplinary action. In particular, disciplinary action cannot be taken against a member who refuses to take any action which would be

[2] [1966] 2 Q.B. 633.

33

an unfair industrial practice on his part or who refuses to take part in any strike or irregular industrial action which has been called by the organisation or anyone else which is not in contemplation or furtherance of an industrial dispute (e.g., a political strike), or to take part in a strike which would amount to an unfair industrial practice on the part of the organisation or persons who called, organised, procured or financed it.

(vii) Except in respect of non-payment of any contribution which the rules require him to pay, no member shall be subject to any disciplinary action unless:

(a) he has had written notice of the charge against him, and has been given a reasonable time to prepare his defence;
(b) he is afforded a full and fair hearing;
(c) a written statement of the findings of the hearing is given to him; and
(d) if the rules provide for an appeal, his appeal has been heard or the time for appealing has expired without his having exercised that right.

The Act does not require that the hearing shall be conducted by an independent body as long as it acts fairly. Thus in *MacLean* v. *Workers' Union*,[3] the plaintiff issued a circular criticising the conduct of the executive committee. The committee itself, acting under the rules, resolved to expel him. It was held that the expulsion was valid, for the committee had acted honestly and in good faith.

(viii) A person's membership shall not be terminated unless he has been given reasonable notice of the proposal to terminate his membership, and the reasons for this.

(ix) No restriction shall be placed on the right of any member to institute, prosecute or defend any proceedings before any court or tribunal, or give evidence in any such proceedings.   **[103]**

Unfair Industrial Practice (section 66)

It is an unfair industrial practice for any organisation of workers, or any official acting on its behalf, to take or threaten to take any action in contravention of the preceding nine principles. If this happens an application may be made to the Registrar under section 81 for him to investigate the matter, or the Registrar may himself investigate on his own initiative under section 83; a case may be presented to the NIRC under section 101 or 103 or 104 or to the Industrial Tribunal under section 107 or 108 (see Chapter 5). The following actions may thus be brought: **[104]**

[3] [1929] 1 Ch. 602.

(a) *By a complainant under section* 101 (to the NIRC)
  (a) It must be shown that the respondent has taken the action complained of;
  (b) that the action was an unfair industrial practice other than under sections 5 (1) or 22; and
  (c) that he is a person against whom the action was taken.

Normally, the person who will complain against a breach of section 65 will be a worker who is a member of an organisation of workers, or who has been refused membership, or who has been expelled, but in theory any person adversely affected by the alleged unfair industrial practice will be able to bring an action if the above requirements are met.

If the NIRC finds that the complaint is well founded, it may provide any of the following remedies:
  (a) an order determining the rights of the complainant and the respondent in relation to the action specified in the complaint;
  (b) an award of compensation to be paid by the respondent to the complainant;
  (c) an order directing the respondent to refrain from continuing that action or any like action in relation to the complainant.

However, if the complaint is against a trade union official, and it is shown that the action was taken in his capacity as a union official within the scope of his authority on behalf of the trade union, the NIRC will not make an order against him under (b) or (c) above. Such remedies, however, will still lie against the trade union itself.

[105]

(b) *By the Registrar under section* 103 (to the NIRC)
  If the complaint is against a trade union, then a member, or former member, or person who has been refused membership or been prevented from obtaining membership, may make an application to the Registrar on the grounds that action has been taken against him which constitutes an unfair industrial practice by virtue of section 66 or that there has been a breach of the rules of the trade union (but not a breach of the rules relating to the application of political funds, or on a vote taken to approve an instrument of amalgamation—in both these cases, alternative remedies exist—see section 115, *post*, page 48): section 81. The registrar will not proceed with the application unless he is satisfied that the person who made the complaint was eligible to make it, and that it was brought within four weeks of:
  (a) the date of the action complained against; or
  (b) the earliest date on which the complainant knew of the action complained of; or

(c) the date when the final determination of the action to which the complaint relates was made by the trade union. He may still decide to proceed with the application, even though the four weeks period has elapsed, if he thinks that in the circumstances it was not practicable for the application to be made before the end of that period. (This will apply, for example, of the complainant was ill, or otherwise not able to pursue the matter at once.)   **[106]**

If, however, the trade union has an adequate appeals procedure which has not been exhausted, the Registrar may defer consideration of the application, but it may be submitted at any time within four weeks from the final determination of the appeal. The Registrar is not required to proceed with any application which he considers to be frivolous or vexatious. After investigation, the Registrar shall give notice of his conclusions to the applicant and the trade union, and if he thinks that the application is well founded, he shall endeavour to promote a settlement. Any communication made to him for this purpose shall not be admitted in evidence in any proceedings before the NIRC or the Industrial Tribunal without the consent of the person who made it. If no settlement is reached, and no complaint is presented to an industrial tribunal under section 107 (below), and if the Registrar considers that the matter is of such a serious character that it ought to be brought before the NIRC, then he shall so bring it. The NIRC may grant the original applicant any of the following remedies, namely:

(a) an order determining his rights and the rights of the trade union in relation to the action complained of;
(b) an award of compensation to be paid to the original applicant by the trade union in respect of the action complained of;
(c) an order directing that the trade union shall refrain from continuing to take such action or other like action in relation to the complainant.   **[107]**

(c) *By the Registrar under section* 104 (to the NIRC)

If the Registrar has reason to suspect that a trade union has committed a serious breach of its rules, or has taken any action in contravention of the principles laid down in section 65, he may, on his own volition, investigate the matter: section 83. (Again this procedure does not apply to any breach of a rule in pursuance of sections 3, 4 or 5 of the Trade Union Act 1913 relating to the restriction of the application of funds for certain political purposes, or a breach of rules in taking a vote on a resolution to approve an instrument of amalgamation or transfer under the Trade Union

(Amalgamation etc.) Act 1964—for which see section 115, *post*, page 50.) If his investigations show that a breach of the rules or action contrary to the principles of section 65 has occurred he will notify the trade union of his conclusions, and endeavour to secure such action as will serve to remedy or mitigate the consequences, and prevent a continuance or repetition of the breach or action in question. If the Registrar fails to receive satisfactory action or an undertaking, and considers that it would be an appropriate case to present to the NIRC, he will inform the trade union that unless he receives an appropriate undertaking or unless remedial action in respect of the matter is taken, he intends to present such a case. If the undertaking or remedial action is still not given or carried out, he shall present such a case to the NIRC under section 104. If the NIRC finds that the action or undertaking given in the notice from the Registrar has not been taken or given, or the undertaking has not been fulfilled, and that there has been a breach of the rules or the principles of section 65, the NIRC may make an order directing the trade union to take such action as the court thinks is requisite to remedy or mitigate the consequences, and to prevent a continuation or repetition of the action or breach.   **[108]**

(d) *By the complainant under section* 107 (to the Industrial Tribunal)

A member of an organisation of workers, or former member (who has not voluntarily resigned) or a person who has sought and been refused membership, or who has been prevented from obtaining membership may apply to the Industrial Tribunal in respect of a complaint against any organisation of workers of an unfair industrial practice under section 66 (breach of the principles of section 65, above) or breach of the rules. This action is different from an action in the NIRC under section 101 (above) in five respects. Firstly, actions in the NIRC may be brought by anyone affected, whereas under section 107 the action is restricted to members, former members who have not voluntarily resigned, and excluded persons. Secondly, an action under section 101 provides for different remedies, as well as certain protections for trade union officials, which do not apply to an action under section 107. Thirdly an action under section 107 can only be brought against an organisation of workers, whereas under section 101 it can be brought against anyone. Fourthly, the amount of compensation payable to an individual under section 107 is limited by section 118 (see page 51, *post*), whereas no such limit applies to an award under section 101. Fifthly, if the complaint under section 107 is against a trade union or an employers' association, the complaint will specify that the action was taken against the complainant, but there is no such requirement if the complaint is against an unregistered body. Thus as long as the complainant is eligible to make the complaint (as a member, etc.) against an unregistered organisation, he may do so in respect of action taken against some-one else.   **[109]**

The complaint will not be entertained by the tribunal if a complaint has also been made to the Registrar under section 81, and the Registrar has not yet given notice of his conclusion. Apart from this if the tribunal finds that there has been a breach of the principles of section 65, or a breach of the rules, it can provide the following remedies:

(a) an order determining the rights of applicant and of the organisation in relation to the action which is the subject of the complaint;

(b) an award of compensation to be paid by the organisation to that person.   **[110]**

(e) *By the Registrar under section* 108 (to the Industrial Tribunal)

If a complaint has been made to the Registrar under section 81 (above) which is well founded, and no settlement has been reached, and the Registrar does not propose to present a case to the NIRC under section 103 above, but it appears that a complaint ought to be presented to the Industrial Tribunal, and that the original applicant has not done so and does not intend to do so, the Registrar may present a case against a trade union to the Tribunal. The procedure and award will be the same as a complaint made under section 107 (above). It should be noted that whenever the Registrar brings an action before the NIRC or Industrial Tribunal it is only in respect of registered organisations.   **[111]**

B. REGISTRATION

Any organisation of workers which:

(a) is independent; and

(b) has power, without the concurrence of any parent organisation, to alter its own rules and to control the application of its own property and funds;

is eligible for registration as a trade union: section 67. A federation of workers' organisations is eligible for registration only if all its constituent or affiliated organisations are trade unions or organisations entered in the special register.   **[112]**

(a) *Provisional registration* **(sections 78–80)**

As soon as is practicable after the passing of the Act, the Registrar will arrange for a provisional register to be established, which will be kept until all the entries therein are cancelled. In it, he will provisionally register every organisation which was registered as a trade union under the Acts of 1871–1964. He will also provisionally register any organisation which applies within six months from the passing of the Act for provisional registration on the grounds that it is a trade union within the meaning of those Acts.   [113]

(b) *Cancellation of entries in the provisional register* **(section 79)**

The register will then consider those organisations which are on the provisional register, and if, within six months, he is satisfied that they are eligible for registration under the Industrial Relations Act he will so register them, issue a certificate of registration, and cancel the entry in the provisional register. If, however, he is not satisfied as to their eligibility, he will serve a notice on the organisation stating this fact. The registrar is entitled to cancel the entry in the provisional register unless within six months from the time of the serving of the notice he is satisfied that the organisation would have to alter its rules to be eligible for registration and is taking all necessary steps for the purpose of altering the rules. If, therefore, the Registrar decides not to cancel the entry, he may serve a notice on the organisation allowing it a further period within which to make the necessary alterations. If, at the end of this time, the organisation does not make a new application, the registrar shall cancel the entry in the provisional register. If it does make a new application in consequence of the change in rules, then the registrar, if he is satisfied as to the test of eligibility, may register the organisation under the Act and cancel the entry in the provisional register. If he still considers that the organisation is not eligible, and refuses to register, the remedy of the organisation is to make an appeal to the NIRC, and if no appeal is brought within the time limit, the registrar may cancel the entry in the provisional register. The registrar will also cancel the provisional entry after an appeal has been made to the NIRC, and register the organisation under the Act or not, as the NIRC decides.   [114]

The effect of an entry in the provisional register does not constitute registration for the purpose of the Act, but an organisation so registered is entitled to the benefits of section 96 (immunity from action based on the inducement of a breach of contract, see para. **[306]**, *post*) section 117 (limits on compensation awards against trade unions, see para. **[147]**, *post*) section 153 (recovery of sums awarded against trade unions and employers' associations, see para. **[123]**, *post*) and section 155 (nomination of persons entitled to receive death benefits, see para. **[123]**, *post*). Further, a worker is entitled to receive the protection of section 5 (see Chapter 7) in respect of his

trade union activities if the organisation is on the provisional register.
[115]

The registrar shall cancel the entry in the provisional register:

(a) if he is requested to do so by the organisation, or

(b) if he is satisfied that it has ceased to exist.

A notice of such cancellation will be published in the London and Edinburgh Gazettes.   **[116]**

(c) *Application for registration under the Industrial Relations Act* **(section 68)**

Any organisation of workers, whether formed before or after the Act, may apply for registration, in a form and manner as the Registrar shall prescribe. Along with the application, shall be sent:

(a) a copy of the rules;

(b) a list of its officers;

(c) the names and addresses of any branches;

(d) if the organisation has been in operation for more than one year, it shall send a return containing;

   (i) its accounts for the previous year;

   (ii) a balance sheet; and

   (iii) copy of the auditors' reports.

If the Register is satisfied that the organisation making the application is an organisation of workers, and that it is eligible for registration as a trade union, and that the above requirements have been complied with, then on payment of the prescribed fee, he shall issue a certificate of registration, which will state whether the trade union is registered as a federation of workers' organisations or not. The name by which it is registered shall not be identical to the name of another organisation registered under the Act, nor so nearly resembling the name of another registered organisation as to be likely to deceive. On receipt of the certificate, the trade union will become a body corporate, known by the specified name, having a perpetual succession and a common seal, bearing its registered name. This means that registration confers legal personality, with all its implications. All the funds and property previously held in trust will vest in the trade union without any further assurance, any liability or obligation to which any person is subject in his capacity of trustee shall be transferred to the trade union, and any legal proceedings which are pending by or against the trustees will automatically be continued against the trade union in its registered name.   **[117]**

As soon as is practicable thereafter, the Registrar will examine the rules of the trade union. If they are defective in that they do not conform to the principles of section 65 (above) or the requirements of the 4th Schedule (rules relating to the constitution and management etc., see below), then the Registrar will serve a notice on the trade union, indicating what alteration is needed to remedy the defect, allowing a reasonable period for the trade union to alter and re-submit them: section 75. If the rules are re-submitted, but the Registrar is still not satisfied that they conform to his original notice, he will allow a further period within which the trade union can alter and re-submit them. Until he is satisfied that the rules are not defective, the Registrar shall not approve of them.   **[118]**

Any organisation which is on the provisional register or which is a trade union, may find it necessary to alter its rules in order to:

(a) become eligible for registration, or
(b) eliminate or amend defective rules as a result of a notice from the registrar under section 75, or
(c) where the organisation has amended the rules, and submitted them to the registrar, where he has served a notice indicating what alterations in the amended rules are needed to remedy a defect, or
(d) in any other case, to secure that the rules are consistent with the principles of section 65, or comply with the requirements of the 4th Schedule.

A number of existing trade unions have restrictions imposed by their rules which impose a certain interval which must elapse before rules can be changed, or proposals for change can be made. For example, in some unions, rules may only be revised every three years. The Act provides that notwithstanding such restriction, the rule-changing procedure can be initiated for the above specified purposes: section 94.   **[119]**

(d) *Cancellation of registration* **(section 76)**

If then, at the end of the time specified above, the Registrar does not obtain a satisfactory set of rules, he may apply to the NIRC for the registration to be cancelled. The NIRC will either:

(a) make an order allowing the trade union a further period in which to alter its rules and submit them to the Registrar; or
(b) make an order directing the Registrar to cancel the registration.

Equally, if the Registrar has failed or refuses to approve the rules, the trade union may make an application to the NIRC, which will make an order that either:

(a) the trade union shall have a further period within which it can alter its rules and submit them to the Registrar; or
(b) the Registrar shall approve the rules as submitted.

The Registrar may also apply to the NIRC for the cancellation of the registration of trade union on the grounds:

(a) that it was obtained by fraud or mistake; or

(b) that by reason of a change in its rules or other change of circumstances, the trade union has ceased to be eligible for registration; or

(c) that the trade union has refused or failed to comply with any other requirement of Part IV of the Act (other than a requirement relating to the rules), and has persisted in the default, despite a notice from the Registrar requiring it to be remedied.

If the application is made on grounds (a) or (b) above and the NIRC finds that the application is well founded, it shall cancel the registration. If the application is made in respect of (c) the NIRC can make an order extending the time for remedying the default, as an alternative to an order directing that the registration be cancelled. The registrar will also cancel the registration under the Act if:

(a) he is requested to do so by the organisation; or

(b) if he is satisfied that it has ceased to exist.

A notice of such cancellation will be published in the London and Edinburgh Gazettes.

Section 157 of the Act provided that no organisation of workers shall be registered in future:

(a) as a company under the Companies Act 1948;

(b) under the Friendly Societies Act 1896;

(c) under the Industrial and Provident Societies Act 1965. [120]

There is a small number of such organisations which are, at present, registered under the Companies Act 1948. Such registration will also be void unless the organisation makes an application to be entered on the special register within six months of the date when the provisions of section 84 come into force (see Chapter 3). Furthermore, if the application is made, and entry on the special register is refused, again, the registration under the Companies Act will be void. However, if the application for entry in the special register is granted, the registration under the Companies Act is valid. The incorporation of any organisation of workers under the Friendly Societies Act, and the Industrial and Provident Societies Act, which was effected before the Industrial Relations Act came into force, shall be void.   [121]

(e) *Application for a winding-up order* (section 90)

If the Chief Registrar has reasonable grounds for believing that a trade union is insolvent, he may appoint an inspector to examine into and report on the union's affairs. The inspector may require the production of any books or documents of the trade union, and may examine on oath any officer, member or employee. If the report confirms the belief that the union is insolvent, the Chief Registrar may present a petition to the High Court for the union to be wound up in accordance with the Companies Act 1948 as an unregistered company.   **[122]**

(f) *Advantages of registration*

The following advantages flow from registration:

(i) Only a trade union may apply to the NIRC for an agency shop agreement (section 11).

(ii) The right of a worker to belong to a trade union and to take part in union activities only applies to those unions registered under the Act or on the provisional register. It will not therefore be an unfair industrial practice to dismiss a worker for "trade union" activities in respect of an organisation of workers which is not registered (section 5).

(iii) A trade union may apply to the NIRC in respect of a defective procedure agreement (section 37).

(iv) A trade union (or panel of unions) may apply for recognition as a sole bargaining agent and enforce a recommendation of the CIR (sections 45 and 49).

(v) A trade union is entitled to ask for and receive information to enable it to bargain effectively (section 56).

(vi) Registration confers legal personality, enabling the union to sue and be sued in its own name, to have a perpetual succession, and its property will vest without any further assurance (section 74).

(vii) A trade union (and its officials) will not be guilty of an unfair industrial practice if, in contemplation of furtherance of a trade dispute, it knowingly induces or threatens to induce a breach of contract (section 96), or if it supports action taken by its members or officials which is an unfair industrial practice by virtue of section 96 (section 97).

(viii) Officials of trade unions will not be subject to certain awards under section 101 (see above, page 33).

(ix) Appropriate limits are set for awards of compensation against trade union funds (section 117).

(x) A trade union may present claims to the Industrial Arbitration Board under sections 125 and 126 (see above, pages 29–30).

(xi) Trade unions may be asked, in certain circumstances, to conduct ballots (e.g., section 144).

(xii) A trade union may present a claim to the IAB under the Terms and Conditions of Employment Act 1959 (7th Schedule).

(xiii) Disorderly conduct in the library of a trade union may be an offence under the Libraries Offences Act 1898.

(xiv) Certain income tax benefits may accrue in respect of interest and dividends earned on union investments or chargeable gains which are devoted to the payment of provident benefits (e.g., superannuation and sickness schemes). Income and Corporation Taxes Act 1970, section 338.

(xv) Members of trade unions may nominate persons entitled to receive certain death benefits payable out of trade union funds.

(xvi) The provisions relating to the recovery of sums awarded in proceedings against registered organisations are somewhat different to those which relate to unregistered organisations: section 153. **[123]**

C. TRADE UNION RULES (Schedule 4)

The rules of a trade union must comply with the following requirements:

(a) *In respect of the management and constitution*

(i) They must contain the name, address of its principal office, and the objects for which the trade union was established.

(ii) They must state if the union has branches, and must indicate the extent to which, and the manner in which, the union has power to control the activities of those branches.

(iii) Provision must be made for the election of the governing body, and its re-election at reasonable intervals, and for the manner in which members of the governing body can be removed from office.

(iv) Provision must be made for the appointment or election of officers, and the manner in which they can be removed.

(v) Provision must be made for the election or appointment of officials (if any) who are not officers (e.g., shop stewards, workplace representatives, etc.) and the manner in which they can be removed.

(vi) The rules must state clearly the powers and duties of the governing body, of the officers, and officials.

(vii) Provision must be made as to the manner in which meetings are to be convened and conducted.

(viii) The rules must specify the manner in which any rule can be amended, altered or revoked.

(ix) The rules must specify any body by which, and any official by whom, instructions may be given to members for any kind of industrial action, and the circumstances in which such instructions may be given.

(x) Provision must be made as to the manner in which (for any purpose) election and ballots shall be held or taken, who is to be eligible for voting, preparatory procedure, the counting and scrutiny of votes and ballot papers, and the procedure for declaring and notifying the results.

(xi) In respect of a federation of workers' organisations, the rules must specify the circumstances in which it has power to enter into agreement on behalf of its constituent or affiliated organisations.

(xii) The rules must state the circumstances and manner in which the trade union can be dissolved.

A trade union shall supply a copy of its rules either free or on the payment of a reasonable charge to any person so requesting.   **[124]**

(b) *In respect of membership*

(i) The rules must specify the description of the persons who are eligible for membership, the procedure for dealing with applications, including appeals against refusal of membership.

(ii) The rules must state:

(a) the contribution payable, or the amount on which it is assessed;

(b) the procedure and penalties in case of default of payment.

(iii) The rules must state:

(a) any description of conduct in respect of which disciplinary action may be taken, by way of suspension, expulsion or otherwise (e.g. a fine);

(b) the nature of the disciplinary action which may be taken in respect of each such description of conduct;

(c) the procedure for taking disciplinary action, and the appeal procedure.

(iv) The rules must specify any other circumstances (and the procedure) whereby membership may be terminated other than by expulsion.

(v) The rules must specify a procedure for enquiring into any complaint of a member in respect of an alleged breach of rules by the trade union or an official.   **[125]**

(c) *In respect of property and finance*

(i) The rules must make provision for the purposes for which the union property and funds are to be applied or invested, and the manner thereof.

(ii) If the union makes financial payments to members, the rules must provide for the amounts of those benefits, and the circumstances in which they are to be made available to members.

(iii) The rules must provide for keeping of proper accounts, and the preparation and auditing of the accounts, and for the rights of members to inspect those accounts and the register of members.

45

L.R.—6

(iv) The rules must provide for the distribution of the union's property and funds in the event of a dissolution.   **[126]**

If there are any special circumstances whereby a particular requirement set out above is inappropriate, the Registrar has power to waive that requirement, and the Schedule will not apply in that case. The failure to fulfil any requirements as set out above shall not invalidate the rules, and shall not confer any right or make available any remedy except as provided by sections 75 and 76 (power of the Registrar to approve the rules, and to apply to the NIRC for cancellation, see para. **[120]**, *ante*).   **[127]**

The legal effect of the rules

The effect of the rules of the trade union is to constitute a contract between the union and its members. In so far as a breach of that contract is concerned, an action can be brought in the High Court. However, if the breach of the rules amounts to a breach of the principles laid down in section 65, this will constitute an unfair industrial practice, and an action by anyone affected can be brought in the NIRC, or (by a member, former member who has not resigned, or person who has been refused membership) in the industrial tribunals. The latter persons may also bring a case in the tribunals in respect of any other action which constitutes a breach of the rules.
[128]

Subject to section 65, and to the approval of the rules by the Registrar, the union will be able to lay down who is to be admitted to membership, and on what terms. The Act merely requires that a person shall not be excluded because of arbitrary or unreasonable discrimination. Clearly, a discrimination based on sex, colour, religion, political beliefs, etc., would be unreasonable. In this connection, it is interesting to look at some of the pre-1971 cases on this subject, to see how they compare with the new law. For example, in *Faramus* v. *Film Artistes' Association*,[4] the rules of the trade union stated that no person convicted of a criminal offence (other than a minor motoring offence) shall be eligible to join or remain a member. In 1938 the plaintiff (then aged seventeen), had been convicted of taking away a motor car without the owner's consent and during the war of an offence against the German occupation of the Channel Islands, for which he was sent to a concentration camp. He subsequently joined the union, and was a member of its national committee when the convictions came to light. The House of Lords held that his admission to the union was a nullity. It is submitted that this decision would no longer be followed, for it is surely unreasonable to hold a conviction of a

[4] [1964] A.C. 925.

high-spirited youth against him for the rest of his life, and the "crimes" against the Germans during their occupation were hardly great enough, to warrant his exclusion from the union. Equally, in *Martin* v. *Scottish Transport and General Workers' Union*,[5] the plaintiff was admitted during the war as a temporary member, though there was no provision in the rules for this class of membership. After the war, his membership was revoked, and he brought an action for a declaration that he was still a member. It was held that as the rules did not provide for temporary membership, he had never actually been a member, and therefore, he could not obtain the declaration he sought. It is submitted that nowadays, in similar circumstances, an action would succeed, for, by refusing to give him full membership in the first place, he had been arbitrarily discriminated against.   **[129]**

If the rules provide that the union will give legal assistance in respect of any matter arising out of the member's contract of employment, the union fulfills that obligation by taking competent legal advice on the member's behalf.[6] Nor does the union break its contract with the members by refusing assistance if the latter fails to show his action would have a reasonable prospect of success.[7] But if the trade union fails in its contractual obligations to provide competent advice, with the result that a member loses the prospects of a successful legal action, an action for breach of contract in the ordinary courts may be brought by the aggrieved member.   **[130]**

The fact that the Registrar has approved the rules does not mean that the trade union will be able to act in accordance with them if that act constitutes a breach of section 65, and a union will not escape liability in any action in respect of an unfair industrial practice merely because it has acted in accordance with the rules. For example, in *Birch* v. *National Union of Railwaymen*,[8] the rules of the union stated that anyone who had contracted out of the political fund was not eligible to hold any office involving the management of that fund. The rule had been approved by the Registrar. The plaintiff was elected to Branch Chairman, an office which involved control over the political fund, and the union declared him to be ineligible for the office, as he had contracted out. It was held that the rules violated the Act of 1913 (see para. **[144]**, *post*) and the plaintiff was entitled to a declaration that he was eligible to be the branch chairman. By parity of reasoning, therefore, a union

---

[5] [1952] 1 All E.R. 691
[6] *Cross* v. *Biska*, [1968] 1 All E.R. 250.
[7] *Buckley* v. *N.U.G.M.W.*, [1967] 3 All E.R. 429.
[8] [1950] Ch. 602.

which violates the principles of section 65 cannot rely on the rules
to justify its action.   [131]

Expulsion from the union

A trade union may only expel a person if it has the power to do
so in its rules.[9] Since the rules are required to specify the conduct for
which any disciplinary action can be taken (above), a member will
only be disciplined if this is within the strict confines of the rule
concerned, and the smallest irregularity in disciplinary proceedings
will often annul them altogether. Moreover, the court will decide
whether or not a breach of the rule did in fact take place, for questions of interpretation of the meaning of the rules is within its
province. Thus in *Lee* v. *Showmen's Guild of Great Britain*,[10] the
plaintiff was expelled from the defendant Guild under a rule designed
to prevent "unfair competition". The court held that the expulsion
was void, for the Guild had misconstrued the meaning of the term.
This will apply particularly in those cases where the conduct specified
in the rules is rather vague, e.g., a rule which permits disciplinary
action "for conduct detrimental to the union."[11] In these cases,
the court will determine whether or not such conduct was detrimental, not the union. In doing so, it will not necessarily be un-
sympathetic to the objects of trade unions and their interests. For
example, in *Evans* v. *National Union of Printing, Bookbinding and
Paper Workers*,[12] the plaintiff absented himself from work on a
number of occasions, contrary to an agreement between the employers and the union. Because of his conduct, the union expelled
him. It was held that the expulsion was valid. It was in the interests
of collective bargaining that the union should do its utmost to ensure
the adherence of its members to the agreement reached with the
employers.   [132]

If the union rules provide for an appeals procedure, that procedure
must in general be followed in respect of any appeal from any disciplinary action.[13] However, if the expulsion is void for lack of
authority, the union appeals machinery cannot cure the defect, and
the member may appeal to the court without going through the
appeals procedure.[14]   [133]

---

[9] *Spring* v. *National Amalgamated Stevadores & Dockers Society*, [1956]
2 All E.R. 221.
[10] [1952] 1 All E.R. 1175. It appears that the Showmen's Guild is not eligible
for registration under the Act as it is a trade protection society rather than an
employers' association.
[11] *Kelly* v. *Natsopa*, 31 T.L.R. 632.
[12] [1938] 4 All E.R. 51.
[13] *White* v. *Kuzych*, [1951] A.C. 585.
[14] *Annamunthode* v. *Oilfield Workers Trade Union*, [1961] A.C. 945.

Since disciplinary action against a member involves a quasi-judicial process, the Industrial Relations Act now insists that the procedure be governed by principles of natural justice, as laid down in section 65 (above).   **[134]**

D. ADMINISTRATIVE PROVISIONS (sections 87-89 and 5th Schedule)

Every trade union shall keep proper accounting records which give a true and fair view of the state of affairs. A satisfactory system of control of its accounting records, cash holdings and receipts and remittances must also be kept. There must also be kept a register of its members in such form as the Registrar may require.   **[135]**

Every trade union shall send to the Registrar an annual return in each calendar year, together with its audited accounts. The return shall be sent before 1st June, and relate to the preceding year. Schedule 5 of the Act contains provisions for the appointment, qualifications, removal and functions of the auditors.   **[136]**

Every trade union shall publish an annual report relating to its activities, and shall either supply a copy to every member free of charge, or include it in a journal relating to its affairs which is available to all members. If a union has a small number of members, the Registrar may exempt it from this provision, if in his opinion it would be unduly onerous for the union to carry it out. In this case, however, the union must provide every member with a free copy of its annual return. Every trade union must supply on the request of any person a copy of its rules, either free or on payment of a reasonable charge.   **[137]**

Part III of the 5th Schedule contains provisions in respect of members superannuation schemes operated by the trade union. **[138]**

A trade union must notify the Registrar of any changes:

(a) in its rules;
(b) in its officers;
(c) in its principal address.   **[139]**

A copy or note of these changes, together with the prescribed fee, must be sent within one month, whereupon the Registrar shall register the change. If the notice relates to a change in the rules, the registrar will examine them, and if they are defective in that they do not conform to the principles of section 65 or the 4th Schedule, he will serve a notice indicating what alteration is necessary to remedy the defect. The amended rules will be treated in the same way as the rules are on registration, i.e., a further reasonable period for alteration can be given, and, if he is still not satisfied, the registrar can apply to the NIRC for the cancellation of registration. Equally, the trade union may apply to the NIRC for a further period within which to alter the rules, or, alternatively, an order from the NIRC directing the registrar to approve the amended rules.   **[140]**

E. POLITICAL FUNDS OF A TRADE UNION

The rules relating to the establishment and application of a political fund by a trade union, which were laid down by the Trade Union Act of 1913, have remained unchanged, and most of that Act is still in force. Its provisions are repeated here for convenience.   **[141]**

A trade union may not use its funds for certain specified political objects (but without prejudice to other political purposes), unless the furtherance of those objects has been approved of by a resolution passed on a ballot by a majority of members. When this happens, the union must have rules, approved of by the Registrar, providing for a separate political fund. Any member who wishes to contract out of this fund shall be able to do so, and a person who has contracted out shall not be excluded from any benefit or disqualified from any office (other than a position connected with the management of the political fund). Contributing to the political fund must not be made a condition of membership of the union.   **[142]**

The specified objects referred to are:

(a) the payment of the expenses of a candidate for a parliamentary or other public office;

(b) the holding of meetings or distribution of literature for such candidates;

(c) the maintenance of such persons holding such office;

(d) the registration of electors or the selection of candidates.

(e) the general distribution of election literature.

If a trade union wishes to engage in any other form of political action it may do so without the necessity of utilising the political fund. A complaint relating to a breach of the rules of the political funds will be governed by the old law on this subject. The Registrar may investigate the matter, and make an order which may be recorded in the county court and enforced as an order from that court. Similarly, a complaint relating to a breach of the rules in taking a vote on a resolution to approve an instrument of transfer or amalgamation may be made to the Registrar under the Trade Union (Amalgamations, etc.) Act 1964. An appeal from his decision in either case will lie to the NIRC: section 115.   **[143]**

F. MISCELLANEOUS MATTERS

(a) *Certification*

Under the Trade Union Act 1913 a trade union could obtain a certificate to the effect that it was a trade union, instead of applying for registration. These provisions have now been repealed, and such certificated organisations (mainly employers' associations) will have to apply either to go on the provisional register or for registration. (They do not go on the provisional register automatically, as the relevant provisions only apply to trade unions which were registered under the old law.)   **[144]**

(b) *The ultra vires doctrine*

As long as the principal objects of an organisation of workers include the regulation of relations between workers and employers it will be able to pursue any other lawful object as provided by its constitution or rules. Any activity not thus authorised is ultra vires and void.   **[145]**

G. LIMITS ON COMPENSATION AWARDS AGAINST TRADE UNIONS (sections 117–118)

In any proceedings before the NIRC where an award of compensation is made against a trade union, the award shall not exceed the appropriate limit as follows:

If the membership of the union is less than 5,000, the limit is £5,000.

If the membership of the union is more than 5,000 but less than 25,000, the limit is £25,000.

If the membership of the union is more than 25,000 but less than 100,000, the limit is £50,000.

If the membership of the union is more than 100,000, the limit is £100,000: section 117.   **[146]**

The compensation limits which can be awarded by the NIRC under section 103 (see para. **[106]**, *ante*), by an industrial tribunal under section 106 (in respect of an action based on section 5 (1) or 22, see Chapter 7), by the tribunal under sections 107 or 108 (see paras. **[110]** – **[111]**, *ante*) shall not exceed:

(a) the amount which represents 104 weeks pay of the complainant; or

(b) 104 × £40 (i.e., £4,160).

whichever is the lesser sum: section 118.   **[147]**

Apart from the appropriate limits mentioned above, there is no limit prescribed in respect of any other action (e.g. one based on section 101, see above, page 11). Thus an individual who is strongly victimised by an unregistered organisation of workers should apply to the NIRC under section 101. If the Registrar brings a case to the NIRC under section 103 or to an industrial tribunal under section 108, or if the individual takes the case to a tribunal under section 107, the compensation is limited by section 118. However, the general principles as to compensation to be adopted is laid down by section 116. This states that in any proceedings before the NIRC or the Industrial Tribunal, the amount of compensation will be such amount as the court or tribunal considers to be just and equitable, having regard to the loss sustained by the aggrieved party, in so far as the loss was attributable to the action taken by the party in default. The loss sustained will include any expenses reasonably incurred in consequence of the matter to which the complaint relates, and the loss of any benefit which he might reasonably be expected to have but for those matters. However, the complainant is under the normal common law duty to mitigate against his loss. For example, in *Edwards* v. *S.O.G.A.T.*,[15] the plaintiff was wrongfully expelled from the union. Because of this he was unable to obtain appropriate employment, and he refused to take various labouring jobs. The Court of Appeal held that he had not acted unreasonably in so refusing, and that he was entitled to £3,500 damages. This sum was considerably in excess of the loss he had suffered due to his being unemployed for some of the time, but the court thought that his chances of promotion, and the fact that it would take him some time to live down his action were relevant factors to be taken into account in assessing his award.   **[148]**

If the complainant has contributed to the matter which is the subject of the complaint, the court or tribunal may reduce the award accordingly as it thinks just and equitable.   **[149]**

Any compensation awarded against a trade union, its trustees or its officials cannot be enforced against the individual property of the trustees, or members of the union, or trade union officials, as the case may be. Nor can the award be enforced against trade union funds which by the rules are precluded from being used for the financing of strikes or other industrial action (section 153). Other than this, any judgment, order or award made against a trade union shall be enforceable against any property belonging to, or held in trust for, the trade union.   **[150]**

---

15 [1970] 1 All E.R. 905.

CHAPTER THREE

OTHER ORGANISATIONS COVERED BY THE ACT

A. ORGANISATIONS OF EMPLOYERS

An organisation of employers is an organisation (whether temporary or permanent) which either (a) consists wholly or mainly of employers or individual proprietors of one or more description and is an organisation whose principal objects include the regulation of relations between employers or individual proprietors and workers or organisations of workers, or (b) is a federation of employers' organisations (section 62). In some respects this definition is wider than the pre–1971 concept of an employers' association, for the Industrial Relations Act states that if a body *includes* as a principal object the specified statutory object of regulating relations between employers and workers or their organisations, it is an organisation of employers. The definition is narrower in that it is confined to those organisations which negotiate with organisations of workers, and trade protection societies and other organisations which have, as their function, the regulation of relations between employers inter se, are now excluded. **[151]**

On the other hand, the new definition doesn't take us very far. There are possibly some 2,000 trade associations which consist mainly or wholly of employers; their functions frequently take them into the area of collective bargaining, but it is not very often that such activities appear as an object of the association concerned, let alone a principal object. Indeed, it may be doubted if such organisations have anything remotely resembling a "principal object", in that their activities are so multifarious and diverse, and change from year to year, that the concept bears little relation to reality. A considerable number of these trade associations are incorporated under the Companies Act, and because such registration would be void if in fact they are trade unions by the old definition (or an employers' association by the new definition), this is avoided by inserting a clause in the objects of memorandum preventing them from exercising any power or pursuing any object which, if an object of the association, would make them trade unions within the old legal definition. Nevertheless, without the power in the objects clause, they continue to exercise the functions! **[152]**

The result is that there are five types of organisations to consider.

Organisations of employers
can be either

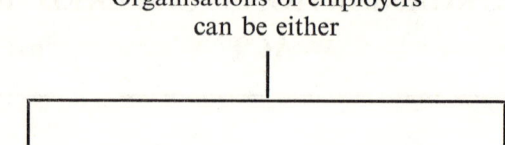

(a) employers' association (regis-   (c) unregistered organisation
    tered)   of employers
(b) federation of employers'   (d) unregistered federation of
    organisation (registered)   employers
        (e) trade associations (which may, or may not,
            or may sometimes, regulate the relations
            between workmen and employers)

An employers' association is defined as an organisation of employers which is registered under the Act as an employers association. If the organisation is so registered, then any registration as a company under the Companies Act 1948, or the Friendly Societies Act 1896, or the Industrial and Provident Societies Act 1965, is void: section 157. There are at least 200 employers' associations which will be affected by this provision. However, an unregistered body (be it an organisation of employers, a federation, or a trade association) can continue to be incorporated under such Acts (in practice, the Companies Act). For the purpose of this chapter, trade associations which exercise collective bargaining functions will be treated as unregistered organisations of employers. If they continue as trade associations, they will not have the protections of the Industrial Relations Act, but may well come within the scope of the Act for some purposes in respect of their activities as organisations of employers. **[153]**

A federation of employers' organisations must consist wholly or mainly of constituent bodies whose principal objects include the regulation of relations between employers and workmen or organisations of workers, *and* is an organisation whose principal objects include the regulation of relations between employers and workers or organisations of workers, *or* include the regulation of relations between its constituent or affiliated organisation. A federation of employers' organisations is eligible for registration, and the Act does not require that all its constituents shall be registered (as is the case with federations of trade unions). The reason is that such federations may consist partly of employers' associations, and partly of trade associations, and as some of the latter may not be able to register themselves, it was though that this should not debar the whole federation from registering.   **[154]**

All organisations of employers (other than federations of employers' organisations), are required to observe certain principles: section 69. Any person who applies for membership, and who is an employer of the description which, in accordance with its rules, the organisation is intended wholly or mainly to consist, shall not be excluded from membership by way of arbitrary or unreasonable discrimination. Further, all such organisations must observe the principles stated in section 65, subsections (3) to (10) (see para. [103], *ante*) in the same way as organisations of workers, and it will be an unfair industrial practice for any organisation of employers, or any official acting on its behalf, to take or threaten to take any action against any member or other person in contravention of any of these guiding principles.   **[155]**

The right of an organisation of employers (or a federation of employers' organisations) to register, and the powers of the Registrar on such an application, and the effect of registration, are the same (with appropriate modifications) as already discussed relating to organisations of workers (see paras. [112] – [119], *ante*).   **[156]**

There are not many employers' associations registered as trade unions under the pre–1971 law (as they are entitled to be if they come within the statutory definition), but those which are registered will be placed on the provisional register automatically. These entries will be cancelled in the same manner as trade union entries are cancelled. While it is on the provisional register, an employers' association is entitled to the privileges which registration confers by virtue of section 96 (protection from an action based on inducing a breach of contract) and 152 (recovery of sums awarded by way of damages against the association).   **[157]**

The power of the registrar to investigate complaints against an employers' association is contained in sections 81–83, and is identical to his powers to investigate trade unions. Equally, the administrative provisions concerning accounts, annual returns, audit and annual report, change of rules and officers, winding up, and offences (sections 87–91) are also the same as in the case of trade unions. The protection given to an employers' association or its officials under sections 96 and 97 are the same as for trade unions, but curiously enough, under section 139 (3) (order of the NIRC to discontinue industrial action in a national emergency—see Chapter

6), only applies to trade union officials, not those of an employers' association. So too, there is no limit on the amount of compensation which may be awarded under sections 101, 107 or 108 in respect of an unfair industrial practice committed by an employers' association. Also applicable are the provisions of the 4th and 5th Schedule, and section 135 (exclusion of illegality on the grounds of restraint of trade). **[158]**

It is necessary to take a brief look at the legal position of those organisations of employers which do not register under the Act. It is unlikely that any such organisation will, on being put on the provisional register, apply to have the registration cancelled, and in so far as some organisations have a certificate under the 1913 Act, this will now be meaningless. Of course, such certificated organisations may apply for inclusion on the provisional register on the ground that it is a trade union within the meaning of the Act, and equally may apply for registration in the manner provided by the Act should it desire to do so. Assuming, therefore, that none of these considerations apply, we will be left with an unregistered organisation of employers, and must establish its legal position under the Act. As with an unregistered organisation of workers, it is excluded from the relevant part of the four principles stated in section 1 (which refers to "the free association of . . . employers in employers' associations, so organised as to be representative, responsible and effective bodies . . .") though why such attributes should not apply to unregistered organisations of employers is not clear. The majority of such organisations will be trade associations, and there is no reason to suspect that these are less likely to be representative, responsible and effective bodies than registered organisations. If the unregistered organisation is already incorporated under the Companies Act, such incorporation will remain unaffected. If it is not incorporated, it will remain an unincorporate association, with no legal personality. However, civil proceedings may be brought by or against it in its name, and any judgment, order or award may be enforceable against any property belonging to it, or held in trust for it, but recovery of such sums awarded by way of compensation or damages, or costs or expenses, shall not be enforceable against funds which, under its rules, are precluded from being used for financing lock-outs or other industrial action: section 154. As with employers' associations, there is no limit to the amount of compensation which may be awarded in respect of any unfair industrial practice (apart from the limit on compensation awarded to a person which is imposed by section 118). An unregistered organisation of employers cannot be a party to an agency shop agreement under the

Act, though there is nothing to prevent such organisation making this type of agreement voluntarily with an organisation of workers. However, any attempt to enforce it (e.g., by inducing the dismissal of a worker who refused to comply with its provisions) would amount to an unfair industrial practice under section 33 (3) (a) (inducing an employer to act contrary to section 5 (2)), for the modification of workers' rights by section 6 (see Chapter 7) only applies to agency shop agreements drawn up between trade unions and employers' associations. However, an unregistered organisation of employers may enter into an approved closed shop agreement, for it was thought that it would be too great a handicap for a trade union to require an organisation of employers to be registered before a joint application could be made for an approved closed shop. It is interesting to note that it is not an unfair industrial practice to take strike or other irregular industrial action to induce an unregistered organisation of employers to join in the making of an application for an approved closed shop agreement, though it would be if such action was directed against an employers' association.   **[159]**

An unregistered organisation of employers may join in the making of an application to the NIRC for an order designating a procedure agreement an exception to the provisions of section 22 (unfair dismissals) and may equally apply for the revocation of that order. The presumptions of sections 35 and 36 (legally enforceable collective agreements) apply to all organisations of employers, but section 37, which deals with remedial action in the event of a procedure agreement being absent or defective, only applies in respect of employers, not their organisations. In other words, section 37 may be used to impose legally enforceable plant agreements, not federated agreements. However, if the CIR makes an extended reference under section 39, it can include an employers' association, but not, apparently, an unregistered organisation of employers. In respect of sections 96, 97 and 98 (see *post*, Chapter 5), an unregistered organisation of employers is in the same position as an unregistered organisation of workers, and equally the protections afforded to the officials of such bodies by section 101 (4) will not apply. Section 135 (exclusion of illegality on the grounds of restraint of trade applies to all organisations of employers, registered or not.   **[160]**

B. ORGANISATIONS ENTERED IN THE SPECIAL REGISTER (sections 84–86)

There is a number of organisations which, although not trade unions by the pre-1971 definition, nevertheless do play a role in representing their members in a bargaining situation. As an example we may cite the Royal College of Nursing, which represents nurses on the Whitley Council for the National Health Service. Since only registered trade unions will obtain the advantages of the Act, in particular in relation to bargaining agencies, such bodies, being unable to register as trade unions, would be prevented from playing a role so far as their industrial relations activities are concerned. The Government decided that this was an undesirable situation, and a special register was set up for the benefit of such organisations, thus enabling them to be brought within the scope of the Act. Such organisations are eligible to register on the special register if they conform to one of two basic conditions. They must be:

(a) already registered under the Companies Act 1948 before the passing of the Industrial Relations Act; or

(b) incorporated by charter or letters patent, whether granted before or after the passing of the Industrial Relations Act.

[161]

If either of these conditions are satisfied, the organisation must also show that:

(a) it is an independent organisation consisting wholly or mainly of workers of one or more descriptions;

(b) *its activities* include the regulation of relations between workers of that description and employers or organisations of employers; and

(c) it has the power, without the concurrence of any parent organisation to alter its own rules and to control the application of its own property and funds. **[162]**

An application for entry in the special register shall be made to the Registrar, together with a copy of the rules, a list of officers, and the names and addresses of its branches (if any). If he is satisfied that the organisation is eligible, he will register it as an organisation of workers other than a federation of workers organisations, and will issue a certificate of registration. It will be noted that it is the activities of the organisation which makes it eligible for registration, whether or not such activities are in accordance with the constitution (as laid down in the memorandum or articles of association or Charter or letters patent) or not. **[163]**

In addition, a federated organisation may apply for inclusion on the special register if:

(a) its membership consists wholly or mainly of constituent organisations or representatives of such;

(b) each of the constituent or affiliated organisations is an organisation which is either a trade union or an organisation which is entered in the special register; and

(c) its activities include the regulations between workers and employers or between workers and organisations of employers.

[164]

It will be noted that there is no requirement that such a federated organisation should, as a precondition of registration, be incorporated as a company, or by charter or letters patent. On being entered in the special register, the organisation will receive a certificate that it is a federation of workers' organisations.   **[165]**

The result is that the special register will consist of organisations of workers and federations of workers' organisations, and any reference to such terms in the Act apply to the organisations in the special register. Thus the Registrar may require the organisation to amend its rules if they do not conform to the principles of section 65 or the 4th Schedule. The Act also states that all the relevant provisions have effect in relation to an organisation in the special register as they have in relation to a trade union. In practice, this means that a specially registered body may apply for a sole bargaining agency, bargaining information, and will be protected from actions based on inducing a breach of contract. At the same time, entry in the special register will bring the organisation within the orbit of the registrar. However, a number of the provisions of the Act do not take effect, because these organisations already possess legal obligations in respect thereof or because they are otherwise inappropriate. These exceptions are as follows:

(a) section 61 (3) defines a trade union as an organisation of workers which is registered as a trade union. The specially registered body is not registered as a trade union: nonetheless, it is entitled to all the privileges which a trade union may possess by virtue or registration;

(b) section 73 deals with the certificate of registration of trade unions. This is otiose in view of section 85 (3);

(c) section 74 deals with incorporation of a trade union and the vesting of its property. This is clearly inapplicable to specially registered bodies, which will already have dealt with these matters, as they will already be incorporated;

(d) sections 78–80 deal with entries on the provisional register of existing registered trade unions;

(e) sections 87–88 deal with administrative provisions which are inapplicable;

(f) section 90 deals with winding up of a trade union, which again is inapplicable.   **[166]**

C. ORGANISATIONS OF WORKERS WHICH ARE NOT REGISTERED AS TRADE UNIONS

(Through the Industrial Relations Act the term "organisation of workers" includes a trade union; reference to a trade union, however, excludes those organisations which have not registered. In the remainder of this chapter, the term organisation of workers will be used to denote only those bodies which have not registered.)

Something must now be said about those organisations of workers which are not registered as trade unions. It must be noted right away that if a body was registered under the Trade Union Acts 1871–1913, it will automatically be placed on the provisional register, where it will stay until the entry is cancelled (see para. **[113]**, *ante*). **[167]**

It has been suggested that a number of existing unions will try to avoid being registered under the Industrial Relations Act by "de-registering" under the old law, and thus they will not be eligible for inclusion on the provisional register. Alternatively, they may request the Registrar to cancel the entry. However, the rules of the union must be looked to, to see if this is possible. For example, a union may have a rule which states that one of its objects is that it shall register as a trade union (this, of course, was a reference to the old law, but it applies equally to the new). If a union tries to de-register contrary to such a rule, any individual member could bring an application for an injunction to restrain the union from acting in breach of the rules. Thus, de-registration would only be possible if the offending rule was itself altered. One way or another, we will find that an unregistered organisation of workers is generally under severe handicaps; it is within the system so far as the restrictive powers of the Industrial Relations Act are concerned, but outside it in respect of most (though not all) of the benefits. **[168]**

An organisation of workers cannot register as a company under the Companies Act 1948, or under the Friendly Societies or Industrial and Provident Societies legislation. In general, it will appear that it will remain an unincorporate association, with no legal personality. To surmount some of the procedural difficulties which this raises, the Industrial Relations Act provides that civil proceedings may be brought by or against such an organisation in its own name. Any award of compensation, damages or costs shall be enforced against the property belonging to, or held in trust for, the organisation, though not against any property comprised in a fund which, according to the rules, is precluded from being used for financing strikes, or other industrial action: section 154. **[169]**

An organisation of workers must conform to the principles laid down in section 65, and failure to do so will be an unfair industrial practice under section 66. However, the registrar will not be able to investigate complaints or alleged breaches of the rules under sections 81 or 83, and it will not be required to submit annual returns and reports under section 88. Nonetheless, the remedy for a complaint of an unfair industrial practice under section 101 still applies, though it is likely that most cases alleging a breach of section 65 or breach of the rules will be taken by the complainant to the Industrial Tribunal under section 107. There is no limit to the compensation awarded which can be made against an organisation of workers but again, in practice the compensation awards will be limited by section 118 (except for cases brought under section 101).   **[170]**

An organisation of workers which is party to a procedure agreement may apply for a designating order under section 31 excluding the operation of the sections on unfair dismissals. It can also enter into a legally binding collective agreement under the provisions of section 34, etc., and sue and be sued thereon. However, it cannot apply under section 37 for a legally binding agreement to be brought into existence where the existing agreement is defective or if one is absent. If, however, such an application is made (e.g. by the employer) and it is referred to the CIR under section 37, the CIR, it will be recalled, may recommend that a larger unit of employment be considered, together with additional parties to the reference. The CIR cannot, apparently, add to that reference an organisation of workers (section 39 (2)).   **[171]**

An organisation of workers cannot apply for a sole bargaining agency under section 45, but an employer may apply that the question as to which organisation of workers shall be recognised as a sole bargaining agent shall be referred to the CIR for examination (section 45 (1) (b)), and the Secretary of State may make a similar application. The CIR may in fact make such a recommendation (section 48 (4)), with or without conditions. However, the recommendation is not capable of being enforced by the ballot procedure under section 49 by or in respect of the organisation of workers. Moreover, if a trade union obtains such an order from the NIRC, but ceases to be a trade union, the order will cease to have effect. If an organisation of workers does manage to obtain sole bargaining rights with an employer, the provisions of sections 51–53 whereby an employee can apply for the discontinuance of a sole bargaining agency do have effect.   **[172]**

An organisation of workers is not entitled to receive information from an employer which may be relevant for bargaining purposes (under section 56), and is not able to present cases to the IAB under sections 125 and 126.   **[173]**

The most serious handicap an organisation of workers will suffer arises under section 96. That section makes it an unfair industrial practice knowingly to induce or threaten to induce a breach of contract in contemplation or furtherance of an industrial dispute, but there is a protection in favour of trade unions and their officials which is not granted to an organisation of workers. Since a strike is prima facie actionable at common law as inducing a breach of contract, it really does not seem to make any difference whether or not the strike is official or unofficial, in breach of an agreement or not. The doctrine in *South Wales Miners Federation* v. *Glamorgan Coal Co.*[1] is clearly revived by the Industrial Relations Act. The result is that any organisation of workers which calls a strike will find it may have to account for its actions before the NIRC under section 101.[2] That an organisation of workers will be caught by the provisions of sections 97 and 98 goes without saying (see paras. **[296]** – **[299]**, *post*). **[174]**

It will be recalled that an individual worker has the right to belong to a trade union (section 5 (1)). He has no such right to belong to an organisation of workers, and consequently he is not protected by section 5 (2) if he is dismissed, penalised or otherwise discriminated against because he joins such a body, or if he is victimised as a result of strike action, or a lock-out (see Chapter 7). On the other hand, the individual has a right not to belong to an organisation of workers, and action designed to compel him to join such a body will be an unfair industrial practice. The agency shop provisions only apply in respect of trade unions, and thus, while an employer will not be guilty of unfair industrial practices if he dismissed, etc., a worker who is not a member of a trade union in such a situation he will be so guilty if he dismisses, etc., a worker on the grounds that the worker is not a member of the organisation of workers with which an agency shop agreement is made. An organisation of workers cannot be considered by the NIRC for an agency shop agreement, or an approved closed shop agreement. **[175]**

It is not an unfair industrial practice to refuse to employ a worker on the grounds that he *is* a member of an organisation of workers; on the other hand, if the refusal is based on the fact that the worker *is not* a member of an organisation of workers, that will be an unfair industrial practice. **[176]**

---

[1] [1905] A.C. 239; see page 92, *post*.
[2] See, however, Chapter 8 for a fuller discussion of this point.

CHAPTER FOUR

THE LAW OF COLLECTIVE BARGAINING

A. THE RIGHT TO BARGAIN (sections 44-50)

The process of collective bargaining refers to negotiations with respect to terms and conditions of employment, or with respect to the making, variation or rescission of a procedure agreement, or with respect to any matter to which a procedure agreement can relate; section 167. Such negotiations are carried out by organisations of workers, on the one hand, and the employer or organisations of employers on the other. **[180]**

At common law, there is no duty on an employer to recognise a trade union[1], or even to bargain with it[2]. Certain nationalised industries have long been under various statutory duties to "enter into" or "to seek" consultations with appropriate trade unions, but these obligations are not thought generally to be legally enforceable. Thus in *Gallagher* v. *Post Office*,[3] the defendants had, for many years, recognised two trade unions for bargaining purposes. It was then decided to withdraw recognition from one of the unions, and an action was brought claiming (*inter alia*) that the withdrawal of recognition amounted to a breach of statutory duty. It was held that the duty on the Post Office was to seek consultations with such organisations as it thought to be appropriate, and did not confer any rights on any particular organisation. In future, however, any order from the NIRC concerning bargaining agency rights shall prevail over such statutory duties as are imposed on the nationalised industries; section 60. **[181]**

The Industrial Relations Act breaks new ground in this respect, by permitting an application to be made by a trade union for recognition as a sole bargaining agent, in respect of a bargaining unit. The "unit" will be those employees of an employer (or two or more associated employers) whose terms and conditions of em-

---

[1] *Thomson* v. *Deakin*, [1952] Ch. 646.
[2] *Stratford & Sons Ltd.* v. *Lindley*, [1965] A.C. 269.
[3] [1971] 3 All E.R. 712.

ployment are, or could appropriately be, the subject of the same negotiations. [182]

An application may be made to the NIRC that the following two questions shall be refered to the CIR for examination, namely,

(i) whether a specified group of employees should be recognised as a bargaining unit or separate bargaining units, and

(ii) whether, in respect of any such bargaining unit, a sole bargaining agent should be recognised, and if so, what organisation of workers or joint negotiating panel should be the sole bargaining agent. The application can be made by:

(a) a trade union;
(b) the employer or associated employers;
(c) the trade union and the employer(s) jointly; or
(d) the Secretary of State. [183]

If the application is made by the trade union or employer, notice of the proposal must first be given to the Secretary of State before the NIRC will entertain it. On receipt of such notice, he will offer such advice and assistance as he may consider to be appropriate with a view to promoting a settlement, and for this purpose, he may refer the matter to the CIR for examination. However, once such notice has been given, the party giving it may proceed with the application to the NIRC. [184]

If the Secretary of State makes the application, he must first consult the employer and any organisation of workers appearing to him to be directly concerned in the matter. It will be noted that although an unregistered organisation of workers cannot make an application, the employer or Secretary of State may do so on its behalf should they so wish, and presumably they will do so if there is a conflict in the unit of employment which requires resolution, and they consider that only the imposition of a bargaining agency scheme by the NIRC can solve it. [185]

If there has been a previous application for a bargaining agency with respect of the same unit, which has resulted in a negative ballot, or if the employees in question have voted for the cessation of the bargaining agency under sections 51–53 (see *post*, page 67) then the NIRC will not entertain any further application in respect of that unit for two years from the date when the ballot was reported to it. If this is not the case, then, as long as the NIRC is satisfied that the parties have endeavoured to settle the issue, and have used the conciliation services available, and that a reference to the CIR is necessary with a view to promoting a lasting settlement, then the issue will be referred to the CIR. The NIRC is not bound to refer any question to the CIR relating to that group of employees which has been considered by the CIR within the previous two years if a further reference would not be justified after so short an interval, but any other question in the reference can still be proceeded with. **[186]**

Once the CIR is seized of the matter, they can, at any time before they make a report, apply to the NIRC to have the reference withdrawn on the grounds that a lasting and satisfactory settlement has been reached, and if the NIRC is equally satisfied, the reference will be withdrawn. Equally, the CIR may decide that it is necessary, for the purpose of achieving a satisfactory and lasting settlement, to extend the reference so as to include other employees (or an associated employer of the employer specified in the reference—but no other employer). If so, they will formulate proposals for such extension, send them to the NIRC, and cause notice of the proposals to be given or published (as appropriate) in order to bring them to the attention of persons who would be affected. Within two weeks from the date of such notice, any persons affected by the proposals may apply to the NIRC to consider whether the proposals are necessary or expedient, and on such application, the NIRC will either:

(a) extend the scope of the reference in accordance with the proposals;
(b) extend it to a lesser extent than proposed; or
(c) direct that the scope remains unchanged.

Failing such application by affected parties, the NIRC shall confirm the proposals and extend the scope of the reference as proposed by the CIR. **[187]**

The CIR will now examine the reference (including any extended reference) and prepare a report, setting out their recommendations. Copies of this will be sent to the Secretary of State, the employers specified in the reference, and to any trade union or organisation of workers which appears to the CIR to be directly concerned. The report will also be published in such a manner as the CIR consider appropriate. **[188]**

For the purpose of determining the bargaining unit, the CIR will take into consideration the extent to which different employees have interests in common, having regard, in particular, to the nature of the work they are employed to do, and their training, experience and professional or other qualifications. The CIR is not permitted to recommend the recognition of an organisation of workers as a sole bargaining agent unless it appears to the CIR that:

(a) the organisation is an independent organisation of workers (i.e. that it is not a "house union"); and

65

(b) that its recognition as sole bargaining agent for that bargaining unit would be in accordance with the wishes of the employees comprised in that bargaining unit, and would promote a satisfactory and lasting settlement to the issue in the reference. In determining whether to make such a recommendation, the CIR will consider:

(a) whether the organisation has or would have the support of a substantial proportion of the employees in the bargaining unit; and

(b) whether it would have adequate resources and is or would be properly organised so as to enable it to represent those employees effectively.

The CIR may also impose conditions in the recommendation, and in particular it may require the organisation recommended as a sole bargaining agent to make sufficient trained officials available for the purpose of bargaining, or to require the organisation to give an undertaking that it will not seek to be recognised as a sole bargaining agent in respect of any other bargaining unit consisting of employees of the employer to whom the recommendation relates. If it appears to the CIR that there are more extensive bargaining arrangements in existence (e.g., a national agreement) the recommendation may specify those arrangements, and be subject to the reservation that the bargaining agent shall not have exclusive negotiating rights in respect of the matters so dealt with.   **[189]**

Once the CIR have made their recommendations, with or without a reservation, then, within six months of the report being sent to the NIRC, the employer or trade union may make an application to the court. No application may be made in respect of an organisation of workers unless it is a trade union, or in respect of a joint negotiating panel unless it is a panel of trade unions. If the NIRC is satisfied that the recommendations of the CIR were unconditional, or that any conditions imposed have been complied with, the NIRC will request the CIR to make arrangements for a ballot to be taken among the employees who comprise the bargaining unit, on the question whether the recommendation of the CIR should be made binding. The CIR can take the ballot itself, or arrange for another body (e.g. the Electoral Reform Society) to supervise it, and will ensure that the ballot is properly conducted and that voting is kept secret. The ballot will not be held until an adequate period has elapsed since the publication of the report. After the ballot has been taken, the CIR will report the result to the NIRC, the trade union or joint negotiating panel, and to the employer.   **[190]**

If the result of the ballot is that a simple majority of the employees voting were in favour of the proposal, then the NIRC will make an order:

(a) defining the unit, and
(b) specifying the employer and trade union, and
(c) directing that from the end of a period of two months, for so long as the order is in force, that trade union or joint negotiating panel shall be recognised as the sole bargaining agent for that bargaining unit (section 50). The order will also specify any extensive bargaining arrangements made in the CIR's recommendations, and be subject to the same reservation. If, while the order is in force, a trade union specified therein ceases to be a trade union, or a joint negotiating panel ceases to be a panel of trade unions, the order will cease to have effect.   [191]

(a) *Withdrawal of recognition of a sole bargaining agent* (section 51)
Any employee who is a member of the bargaining unit may make an application to the NIRC, stating that an organisation of workers which has been recognised by the employer or is required to be recognised as a result of a NIRC order does not adequately represent the employees in that bargaining unit, or a particular section of it to which he belongs. If there is no order for the time being in force under section 50, the NIRC will not entertain the application unless it is supported by not less than one-fifth of the employees in the bargaining unit who have expressed their support for the application in writing. This will apply where the employer has conceded a sole bargaining agency without an order from the NIRC. There may be some difficulties here, in that the dissatisfied employees may not, as a group, be able to muster the necessary one-fifth to make a successful application, because of their numerical inferiority. The Act, therefore, neither helps nor hinders them should they desire a change of bargaining agent. If the sole bargaining agency does exist by virtue of an order from the NIRC, then the application will not be entertained unless:

(a) the application is made at the end of two years from the date of the order, and
(b) the court is satisfied that not less than two-fifths of the employees comprising the bargaining unit have signified their consent in writing.   [192]

Provided therefore that the above conditions are satisfied, the NIRC will direct the CIR to examine the matter, and they will promote and assist such discussions as might lead to a settlement, being allowed a reasonable time for this. If, at the end of this time the application has not been withdrawn, the NIRC, with a view to testing the grounds of the application shall request the CIR to consider whether a ballot should:

(a) extend to all employees within the unit, or
(b) to a limited section of that unit,

and the conclusions on these points will be reported to the NIRC. The CIR will also decide whether to take the ballot themselves, or place it under the supervision of some other body, and will make such arrangements as are necessary to ensure a properly conducted secret ballot. The CIR will then proceed to arrange a ballot in accordance with these conclusions. If the ballot is to extend to all the employees in the unit, the question on it will be whether the trade union (or panel) shall cease to be the bargaining agent for that unit. If the ballot is limited to a particular section of the unit, the question will be whether the agent shall cease to represent that section of the unit. The results of the ballot will then be reported to the NIRC, the applicant, the employer and trade union concerned.   [193]

If the majority of those who voted were in favour of the proposal that the trade union shall cease to be the bargaining agent for the unit, or section of it, as the case may be, then the NIRC shall make an order directing the employer:

(a) to cease to recognise the organisation of workers as the bargaining agent for the unit or section thereof as the case may be, and
(b) not to recognise it as a sole bargaining agent for the unit or section at any time for two years following the date on which the result of the ballot was reported to the NIRC.

Any previous order will be revoked or varied, as the NIRC considers to be appropriate. However, the revocation order will only apply to that organisation of workers in respect of those employees. It is quite possible for another trade union to come along and apply for a bargaining agency in the usual way.   [194]

(b) *Unfair industrial practices* (see **Chapter 5**)
The Act contains six unfair industrial practices in connection with the above.   [195]

(i) Once a trade union or an employer, either separately or jointly, have, with a view to making an application to the NIRC, given notice to the Secretary of State, then the whole matter becomes a pending issue, and remains so until:

(a) the NIRC decides not to refer it to the CIR;
(b) the reference to the CIR is withdrawn; or
(c) six months from the date when the report of the CIR is sent to the NIRC.

It will also remain pending while the Secretary of State is considering it (when no application has been made to the NIRC) until he certifies the date on which:

(a) an agreement was reached; or
(b) no agreement was likely to be reached without an application being made to the NIRC.

While the matter is thus pending, it will be an unfair industrial practice for the employer to organise, etc., a lock-out, or for any person to call, etc., a strike or irregular industrial action (the Act must be read as if the words "relating to that pending question" were included"): section 54.   **[196]**

(ii) Where the NIRC has made an order under section 50 defining the bargaining unit and specifying that the employer shall recognise a particular trade union as the bargaining agent, it will be an unfair industrial practice for the employer:

(a) to carry on any collective bargaining in relation to that unit with any other organisation of employees; or
(b) not to take such action with a view to carrying on collective bargaining with that trade union as might reasonably be expected to be taken by an employer ready and willing to carry on such bargaining: section 55 (1).

In the latter case, however, the normal remedies under section 101 do not apply. Instead, the NIRC can authorise the presentation of a claim to the IAB under section 125 (see para. **[93]**, *ante*) specifying the date on which the unfair industrial practice first occurred; section 105 (5).   **[197]**

Also, it will not, of course, be an unfair industrial practice under (a) if the order of the NIRC mentioned relates to a joint negotiating panel, and the employer bargains with a union on that panel in pursuance of an agreement whereby the panel has consented to his carrying on such bargaining: section 55 (2). Nor will it be an unfair industrial practice if the employer takes part in those more extensive bargaining arrangements which are the subject of a reservation in the NIRC order.   **[198]**

(iii) Where the NIRC has made an order under section 50 defining the bargaining unit and specifying that the employer shall recognise a particular trade union, and that order is still in force, it shall be an unfair industrial practice for any person:

(a) by calling, etc., a strike, or threatening to do so, or
(b) by organising, etc., any irregular industrial action, or threatening to do so,

knowingly to induce or attempt to induce the employer specified in the order to bargain with any other organisation of workers, or not to bargain with the sole bargaining agent: section 55 (3).   **[199]**

Thus, once the NIRC has decided the bargaining structure for the unit, the matter now becomes a closed issue, and action by either side designed to upset the effect of the order of the NIRC is wrongful.
[200]

(iv) At any time within two years from the time when the CIR sent to the NIRC a report under section 48 (whether or not the NIRC has made an order under section 50) it shall be an unfair industrial practice for any person (including a trade union or other organisation of workers or their officials) to call, etc., a strike, or to organise, etc., any irregular industrial action, in order knowingly to induce or attempt to induce an employer to recognise, as sole bargaining agent for the bargaining unit to which the report relates, an organisation which was not recommended for such recognition in that report or knowingly to induce the employer to carry on any collective bargaining with an organisation of workers which was not recommended by that report: section 55 (6). In other words, once the CIR has made a report on the issue, even though no-one has applied for it to be binding, and no ballot has been held, the report will have a two year sanction behind it.[4] If therefore, the report is considered to be unsatisfactory in this respect by some persons, the only remedy is to get the trade union or the employer to challenge the findings of the CIR in the NIRC by means of a ballot.   **[201]**

(v) If the NIRC has made an order under section 53 that a sole bargaining agency shall cease for two years, it will be an unfair industrial practice for any person (including a trade union or other organisation of workers or their officials) to call, etc., a strike, or to organise, etc., irregular industrial action in order knowingly to induce or attempt to induce an employer not to comply with the order: section 55 (7).   **[202]**

(vi) It shall be an unfair industrial practice for an employer by instituting, etc., a lock-out, or threatening to do so, knowingly to induce or attempt to induce any person to refrain from asking an application under section 45 (for a sole bargaining agency) or section 51 (cessation of a sole bargaining agency).   **[203]**

---

[4] But the employer does not commit an unfair industrial practice if he choses to ignore the recommendation and the remedy for a trade union is to apply to the NIRC for a ballot.

B. DISCLOSURE OF INFORMATION FOR BARGAINING PURPOSES (section 56)

For the purpose of all stages of collective bargaining it shall be the duty of an employer to disclose to trade union representatives such information relating to his undertaking as is in his possession and is both:

(a) information without which the trade union representatives would be to a material extent impeded in carrying on collective bargaining with the employer; and

(b) information which it would be in accordance with good industrial relations practice that the employer should disclose to them for bargaining purposes.   **[204]**

In determining what is good industrial relations practice, regard will be had to the principles set out for this purpose in the Code of Industrial Relations Practice (see *ante*, page 2) to be published by the Secretary of State, but that code will not necessarily exclude any other evidence as to what that practice is. If the trade union representatives so request it, the information shall be given or confirmed to them in writing. This, however, does not give the union representatives the right to see any document or to require the compilation of any information which would involve work or expenditure out of reasonable proportion to its value for bargaining purposes. Further, the employer is not required to disclose any information:

(a) the disclosure of which would be contrary to the interests of national security;

(b) which could not be disclosed without contravening a prohibition imposed by an Act of Parliament (e.g. the Official Secrets Act);

(c) which has been communicated to him in confidence;

(d) relating specifically to an individual, unless that disclosure could not be expected to be seriously prejudicial to him, and he has consented to it being disclosed;

(e) the disclosure of which would be seriously prejudicial to the interests of the employer's undertaking for reasons other than its effect on collective bargaining.

(f) any information obtained by the employer for the purpose of bringing, prosecuting or defending any legal proceedings: section 158.   **[205]**

If the employer fails in this duty to provide the trade union representatives (which term includes trade union officials or others

71

who are authorised by or on behalf of the union to carry on the collective bargaining) then a complaint may be presented to the NIRC under section 102. If the complaint is well founded, the NIRC may make any or all of the following orders:

(a) an order determining the rights of the trade union and the employers in relation to the matter complained of;

(b) an order directing that the employer shall take such action in performance of its duty as the court thinks is within his power, being action which in the circumstances he ought to take;

(c) an order authorising the presentation of a claim to the IAB under section 126 (para. [93],, *ante*). If the latter order is made the claims, which will be in writing, will specify the employees in respect of whom it is made, and will ask that certain terms and conditions shall be observed by the employer specified in the claim. The IAB will either allow that claim, or direct that the employer shall observe other terms and conditions which it thinks to be more appropriate. Such terms and conditions will become implied terms of the contract of those employees, and shall have effect until they are superseded or varied by agreement or a subsequent award by the IAB. The award may be backdated, but not earlier than the time at which the NIRC found the employer in breach of his duty under section 56.   **[206]**

The duty to make such disclosure only applies to plant bargaining situations, i.e., as between an employer and one or more trade unions. There is no such duty imposed by the Act in respect of federated or national collective bargaining.   **[207]**

C. CLOSED SHOP AND AGENCY SHOP

(a) *Approved closed shop agreements* **(sections 7, 17 and 1st Schedule)**

A pre-entry closed shop is a system whereby before a worker can obtain employment, he must have a trade union membership card. In some industries, this virtually makes the union an employment agency, for it is easier for the employer to obtain union workers from this source. A post-entry closed shop permits a worker to apply to join the union immediately he obtains employment. It was the original intention of the Government to ban all closed shop agreements, and make them void, but the system has special merit in certain sectors of employment, notably in respect of actors, musicians and seamen. In consequence, a partial exemption has been made in favour of certain post-entry closed shop agreements.   **[208]**

Section 7 provides that any provision in any agreement which precludes an employer from engaging workers who are not members of a trade union or other organisations of workers, or who are not members of a particular trade union or other organisation of workers, shall be void. To this rule, there are two exceptions. Firstly, an agency shop agreement (see page 75) is not rendered void by section 7. Secondly, section 17 and the 1st Schedule lay down the procedure for obtaining an approved closed shop agreement, and if that procedure is followed, the agreement will be valid.   [209]

The Act defines an approved closed shop agreement as an agreement made between one or more trade unions and one or more employers or an organisation of employers, whereby it is agreed that in respect of every such worker covered by the agreement, his terms and conditions of employment shall include a condition that he shall be a member of that trade union, or pay an appropriate contribution to a charity. In addition, the agreement must be approved by the NIRC: section 17.   [210]

The procedure for obtaining an approved closed shop follows the familiar pattern. One or more employers, or an organisation of employers, may make an application jointly with one or more trade union to the NIRC, with a draft of the proposed agreement. The NIRC will not entertain the application if it is made within two years of a similar application, or if a negative ballot has been taken within the previous two years by workers of a description specified in the application. If this does not apply, the NIRC will send the application to the CIR for examination. The CIR must satisfy itself that it is necessary for those workers to have a closed shop agreement for the purposes of:

(a) enabling them to be organised or to continue to be organised as mentioned in section 1 (1) (c) (para. [1], *ante*);
(b) maintaining reasonable terms and conditions of employment and reasonable prospects of continued employment;
(c) promoting or maintaining stable arrangements for collective bargaining relating to those workers;
(d) preventing collective agreements from being frustrated. [211]

The CIR must satisfy themselves on all four points, and in addition must consider whether these purposes could not reasonably be fulfilled by means of an agency shop agreement. A report will then be made by the CIR, which will be sent to the NIRC with copies to the Secretary of State and the applicants. It may also be published. If the CIR is not satisfied on any of the above-mentioned points, it will indicate this in its report, and the NIRC will not proceed further with the application. If however, the report is in favour of an approved closed shop agreement, the NIRC will make an order

allowing between one to three months for an application for a ballot
to be held.   [212]

If there is no effective application for a ballot, the NIRC will
make an order approving the proposals as embodied in the draft
agreement. However, any of the workers to whom the proposed
agreement would have applied on the date of the original application
to the NIRC may make an application for a ballot, but this must be
accompanied by the written concurrence of one-fifth of the relevant
workers. The NIRC will then request the CIR to hold a ballot on
whether or not the proposed agreement shall be made. If either (a)
a majority of the workers eligible to vote or (b) a two-thirds majority
of those actually voting, have voted in favour of the proposed
agreement, then the NIRC will make an order approving the proposals made in the draft agreement. Thus, if there are 1000 workers
to be balloted, to satisfy condition (a), there must be at least 501
in favour of the agreement. In practice, it is likely that condition
(b) will be the relevant one, i.e., a two-thirds majority of those
actually voting will be required before the NIRC will make the
necessary order. If the requisite majority is not obtained, the NIRC
will not approve the proposals, and the matter is now closed for
two years from the date when the result of the ballot was so reported
to the NIRC. No further application can be made in that time relating in whole or in part to workers to whom the original application
related. If an approved closed shop agreement is made between a
trade union and an organisation of employers, and is expressed to
be made on behalf of particular employers, the latter will be bound by
it. If it is not so expressed, then the agreement will bind all employers
who are members of the organisation, whether they were members
at the time the agreement was made or not. A non-federated employer
may always apply to be included in the agreement should he so
desire.   [213]

Once an approved closed shop agreement is in force, a worker to
whom the agreement applies has no right to refuse to be a member
of the relevant trade union despite the provisions of section 5 (1) (b).
An exception is made for conscientious objectors, who may agree
to pay an appropriate contribution to a charity. Such a person
becomes "specially exempt", and provisions similar to those which
apply to such persons under agency shop agreements (below)
apply accordingly. Further, it no longer becomes an unfair industrial practice for an employer to dismiss, penalise or otherwise
discriminate against a non-unionist (except one who has been
specially exempted on conscientious grounds), or to refuse to employ
a person on the grounds that he is not a member of the trade union,
or has refused to become one.   [214]

Discontinuance of an approved closed shop agreement

Once an approved closed shop agreement is in force, any worker to whom the agreement applies may make an application to the NIRC for a ballot on whether or not the agreement shall continue. The application must be supported by the written concurrence of one-fifth of the workers so covered by the agreement. If a ballot was held to establish the agreement, or if a ballot has previously been held on the discontinuance question, two years must elapse from the time the result was reported to the NIRC by the CIR before any further application can be entertained. If these hurdles are surmounted, the NIRC will request the CIR to arrange for a ballot to be taken, and the result will be reported to the applicant, the employer and the trade union. If a majority of those eligible to vote or a two-thirds majority of those voting do not vote in favour of the continuance of the agreement, the NIRC will revoke the previous order, and the agreement shall cease to be an approved closed shop agreement.   **[215]**

Unfair Industrial Practice (**section 33 (3)**)

It will be an unfair industrial practice for any person (including a trade union or organisation of workers or their officials) knowingly to induce or attempt to induce an employer to comply with any closed shop agreement contrary to the Act, by:

(a) calling, etc., a strike, or threatening to do so, or
(b) organising, etc., irregular industrial action short of a strike, or threatening to do so.   **[216]**

It will also be an unfair industrial practice to use such means knowingly to induce an employer or an employers' association to join in the making of an application to the NIRC for an approved closed shop agreement. However, it does not appear to be an unfair industrial practice knowingly so to induce an unregistered organisation of employers to join in the making of an application for an approved closed shop agreement!   **[217]**

(b) *Agency shops* (**sections 6, 8–16**)

The Act, however, does approve of the agency shop agreement, which is defined as an agreement between an employer and one or more trade unions whereby the employer agrees that in respect of the specified workers, their terms and conditions of employment shall include a condition that the worker must either:

(a) become a member of one of those trade unions; or
(b) agree to pay to that trade union (without becoming a member) an appropriate contribution, or, in certain circumstances, agree to pay an equivalent contribution to a charity.

An agency shop agreement may also be made between one or more trade union and an employers' association. If such an agreement is expressed to be made on behalf of the employers specified therein, then those employers will be bound by it. If no such employers are so specified, then the agreement will apply to all the employers who are members of the employers' association, whether they were members on the date the agreement was made or not. Resignation from the employers' association, therefore, will release an employer from the agreement, unless he is one of the employers expressly specified therein as being an employer on whose behalf the agreement was made: section 6 (6). **[218]**

(i) Appropriate contribution

Thus, where an agency shop can be established, the worker is given the choice of joining the trade union, or paying to it what amounts to the equivalent of his union subscription. The appropriate contribution may be made by periodic payments, or periodic payments together with an initial payment, according to the particular agency shop agreement, and, subject to the Act, the agreement will determine the amounts payable. If the payments are periodic, the appropriate contribution shall not exceed the amount the worker would have to pay if he were a member of the trade union, excluding any contribution he would not be required to pay on giving the requisite notice, e.g., contributions to the political levy fund. The initial payment shall not exceed the sum, if any, required by the rules of the union to be paid by a new member. **[219]**

If the worker requests his employer to deduct from his earnings the appropriate contribution and pay this to the trade union (i.e., the check-off system), then as long as that request is in force, any failure on the part of the employer to comply with that request shall not be regarded as a failure on the part of the worker to pay the contribution. If a worker is already employed in the unit of employment when an agency shop agreement comes into force, he will not be required to make any contributions for three months after the date of the agreement; in respect of a worker who is employed subsequent to the agreement being concluded, he will have one month's grace before making any contribution. The Secretary of State has power to make regulations in respect of certain industries substituting shorter periods for the three and one month mentioned. Thus in the construction industry, and the acting profession, it is not infrequent that the employment will have ended before the one month period is up, so far as new employees are concerned. The Secretary of State will no doubt provide for these and similar instances. **[220]**

(ii) Conscientious objectors

If a worker to whom an agency shop agreement applies objects, on conscientious grounds, to joining a trade union and to paying a contribution to it in lieu of membership, he may propose that he shall pay an equivalent contribution to a charity to be determined by agreement between him and the trade union. If this proposal is agreed to by the union, such payments to the charity become the equivalent contribution for the purpose of the Act.   [221]

A worker who makes such an appropriate contribution (either to the trade union or the charity) obtains no rights as against the union based on its rules. Thus, he cannot call upon trade union officials to represent him in any dispute (e.g., before the management's disciplinary board, or before an industrial tribunal) and he is not entitled as of right to avail himself of any of the services provided by the trade union (e.g., legal aid or advice). Nor is he automatically entitled to the benefits of trade union activity, e.g., a wage increase negotiated by trade union representatives, unless his contract of employment contains an express or implied term to that effect.
[222]

(iii) Settlement of disputes

Where a worker claims that he is being required to pay, under the above provisions relating to an agency shop or approved closed shop agreement, a contribution which:

(a) is not payable in accordance with the agreement; or
(b) exceeds the limits laid down in respect of the periodic or initial payments

he may refer the matter to the Industrial Tribunal for determination.
[223]

Similarly, if there is a dispute between a worker and a trade union about:

(a) whether his objections to paying the contribution to the trade union are genuine objections on the grounds of conscience, or
(b) to which charity the contribution would be payable, or
(c) the amount of the contribution which would be equivalent to the appropriate contribution,

the matter is also referable to the Industrial Tribunal for determination. The Act does not lay down any guidelines for the Industrial Tribunal in respect of what does, and what does not, amount to conscientious objections, and presumably the tribunals will adopt individual approaches until the NIRC gives a ruling on the matter. It is probable that the phrase will be restricted to objections of a religious nature, and that social and political grounds will be excluded. There is, after all, a distinction between convictions and

77

conscience, although the line which divides these two concepts are not easy to draw. Thus, supposing a Roman Catholic refuses to join or contribute to a trade union which is dominated by communists. Is this a conscientious objection, or one based on conviction? It is generally thought that the conscience clause would apply to such persons as Jehovah's Witnesses, Plymouth Brethren, etc.   [224]

(iv) Formation of agency shops **(section 11)**
An agency shop may be established by the employer and a trade union by agreement. Failing such agreement, then an employer or the trade union or joint negotiating panel of trade unions may apply to the NIRC, specifying:

(a) the description of the workers in question, and
(b) the employer and trade unions who would be parties to the agreement (if it were made).   **[225]**

The NIRC is precluded from dealing with the matter if:

(a) it is in respect of a unit of employment which has already balloted on the agency shop issue, and the result of the ballot was unfavourable, and an order denying the agency shop was made within the last two years, or
(b) a ballot to discontinue the agency shop has been held and was successful and the NIRC rescinding the agreement within the past two years.

Otherwise if it is satisfied that the trade union concerned is recognised by the employer as having negotiating rights in respect of those workers or rights corresponding to negotiating rights, it shall send the matter to the CIR for action.   **[226]**

The CIR will first examine whether or not the question of sole bargaining agency under section 45 (*ante,* page 63) ought to be settled, on the grounds that until it is, the agency shop agreement is likely to be ineffective or subject to dispute. If they find that this is so, they will report accordingly to the NIRC, which presumably will refuse to grant the application. Subject to this, the CIR will arrange for a ballot to be taken. They will have to decide:

(a) whether the ballot will extend to all the workers falling within the range of the application, or only a limited number, and
(b) whether the ballot shall extend to other workers not covered in the application, but in respect of whom the trade union has negotiating rights, and report accordingly to the NIRC.

The CIR will also decide whether to conduct the ballot themselves, or arrange for another body to do so, and in either case, to make arrangements for a properly conducted secret ballot. After the ballot has been held, the result will be reported to the NIRC, the employer and the trade union.   [227]

If either: (a) a majority of those eligible to vote, or (b) a two-thirds majority of those actually voting, vote in favour of the agency shop, then it will be the duty of the employer to enter into an agency shop agreement in respect of the workers comprised in the ballot, and to carry out such agreement for so long as it is in force. Failure to do so enables the trade union to make an application to the NIRC under section 102 (para. [328], *post*) which may make an order determining the rights of the trade union and employer, and an order directing the employer to take such action in fulfilment of his duty as the court thinks he can and ought to take. A trade union may also take strike or other action against a recalcitrant employer: section 16 (2) (a).   [228]

If the majority of those eligible to vote have not voted in favour of the agency shop or a two-thirds majority of those actually voting have not voted in favour, then the NIRC will make an order directing that:

(a) no agency shop agreement shall be entered into by the employer and the trade union in respect of those workers who were balloted for two years from the date the result of that ballot was reported by the CIR to the NIRC; and

(b) any agency shop agreement purported to be made during that period shall be void.   [229]

Further, the NIRC will not entertain any further application for an agency shop agreement relating in whole or in part to those workers who were balloted for two years.   [230]

Unfair Industrial Practice (**section 13 (2)**)

It is an unfair industrial practice for any person (including a trade union or other organisation of workers or their officials) by calling or threatening to call a strike, or organising industrial action short of a strike, knowingly to induce or attempt to induce an employer *not* to perform a duty imposed on him to enter into an agency shop agreement.   [231]

(v) Discontinuance of an existing agency shop (**section 14**)

At any time when an agency shop is in existence, any worker to whom the agreement applies may make an application to the NIRC for that agreement to be discontinued. The application must have the written support of one-fifth of the affected workers, and if the agreement came about as a result of an order of the NIRC (above), the application will not be entertained for two years from the time the result of the ballot has been reported, as above. If the application is otherwise admissible, the NIRC will request the CIR to hold a ballot, which they will do in the manner mentioned above, and ensure the necessary arrangements for secrecy, etc., are made. The result will then be reported to the NIRC. If a majority of those eligible to vote or two thirds of those actually voting have not voted in favour of the continuance of the agency shop agreement the NIRC will make an order rescinding the agreement, and will not hear any further application in relation to an agency shop in respect of part or all of those workers for two years.   **[232]**

Unfair Industrial Practice **(section 16)**

(i) It will be an unfair industrial practice for an employer, by instituting, carrying on, procuring or financing a lock-out, knowingly to induce or threaten to induce a trade union or any other person to refrain from making an application for an agency shop agreement under section 11, or to refrain from making an application for the discontinuance of the agreement under section 14.   **[233]**

(ii) It will be an unfair industrial practice for any person (including a trade union or other organisation of workers or their officials) by calling or threatening to call a strike or organising irregular industrial action knowingly to induce an employer to enter into an agency shop agreement after an application has been made in respect of the relevant workers under section 11. However, it is not an unfair industrial practice to call or threaten to call a strike, or to organise irregular industrial action short of a strike if the employer fails in his duty to enter into an agency shop agreement contrary to the wishes of the majority of the workers as expressed in the ballot.   **[234]**

(iii) It will be an unfair industrial practice for a trade union to call or threaten to call a strike or to organise irregular industrial action in an attempt to induce an employer not to make an application under section 11.   **[235]**

However, it does not appear to be an unfair industrial practice to take strike or other irregular industrial action to compel an employer to dismiss a worker who has refused or has failed to make his appropriate payments, and it is important that the agency shop agreement deals with this situation. Thus, supposing a contributing member fails to make his appropriate contribution in a particular week. In theory, the employer can dismiss him (see section 6 (2) (b)). If he fails to do so, the trade union may call a strike to compel the dismissal. Since section 8 deals with the appropriate contribution in a way which makes it equivalent to the trade union subscription, it would seem sensible for the agency shop agreement to permit the contributing non-member the same lattitude in falling behind with his contributions as the rules of the trade union make in respect of members. The agency shop agreement will in all probability be a legally enforceable contract, and it is necessary to ensure that both sides observe its terms without resort to provocation of industrial action. Similarly, the agreement should deal with the method of payment to be made to a charity, and the evidential requirements of this.   [236]

D. THE LEGAL EFFECT OF COLLECTIVE AGREEMENTS (sections 34–36)

Collective bargaining is a complex process. It may involve a single trade union or organisation of workers, or a joint negotiating panel of several such organisations. There may be a single employer, or a group organised in an employers' association, or organisation of employers. The contents of the agreement may be of national application, or local, or apply to a particular firm. As well as applying to the participant, non-federated employers may be obliged to comply with its requirements, and workers who are not members of the organisation of workers which negotiated it, may find themselves the recipients of its benefits. Strangely enough, although the Industrial Relations Act makes important provisions in regard to the contractual nature of a collective agreement, it is silent on its normative effect, and in relation to this the pre-1971 law will still apply[5].   [237]

A collective agreement may be defined as any agreement or arrangement, whether written or oral, which:

(a) is made by or on behalf of one or more organisation of workers, and one or more employers, or organisation of employers; and

(b) deals wholly or in part with the terms and conditions of employment of workers, or is a procedure agreement, or both.
                                                                   [238]

In addition, the term "collective agreement" applies to the following cases:

(a) any legally binding decision of any joint body consisting of representatives of organisations of workers and representatives of one or more employer or organisation of employers, established by a collective agreement, for regulating the terms and conditions of employment of workers, or for determining any matter for which a procedure agreement can provide: section 35. Thus plant bargaining is brought within the scope of the Act.

[5] See page 89, below, and Chapter 8.

(b) Any procedure agreement which has been turned into a legally enforceable agreement by virtue of an order of the NIRC under the provisions of section 41 (see below).   **[239]**

A procedure agreement means so much of a collective agreement as relates to:

(a) machinery for consultation with regard to, or for the settlement by negotiation or arbitration of, terms and conditions of employment;
(b) machinery for consultation with regard to, or for the settlement by negotiation or arbitration of, other questions arising between one or more employers and one or more workers or organisations of workers;
(c) negotiating rights;
(d) facilities for officials of trade unions or other organisations of workers;
(e) procedures relating to dismissals;
(f) procedures relating to other matters of discipline;
(g) procedures relating to grievances of individual workers.

[240]

(a) *The contractual effect of collective agreements* (**sections 34–36**)

Section 4 of the Trade Union Act 1871 (now repealed) provided that an agreement between one trade union and another was not directly enforceable at law. Since the same Act defined an employers' association in the same terms as a trade union, this has meant that "federated" agreements, made between an employers' association and a trade union were unenforceable. The section could not apply to plant agreements made between a trade union and a single employer, and these were potentially binding. The 1871 Act has been repealed, so the provision is no longer applicable. However, in recent years, another ground for the non-enforceability of all such agreements held sway. This view fastened on the legal rule that before a valid contract could come into existence in any sphere of activity, the parties thereto had to intend that the agreement was one which would have legal consequences. Transposed into the field of industrial relations, the proponents of this view argued that neither trade unions nor employers desired collective bargains to have legal consequences, and hence, it was argued, they did not intend to create a legally binding contract. A minority of commentators disagreed with this theory on a number of grounds, but chiefly on the difficulty in ascertaining the "intentions" of the bargainers at any particular point in time, and the somewhat artificial nature of the whole concept. In several early cases, the argument was not presented, and the binding nature of a collective agreement was established, but more recently, in *Ford Motor Co.* v. *A.U.E.F.W.*[6], the "no intention" theory was upheld, though the decision is not without its critics.   [241]

In order to clarify the position, the Industrial Relations Act provides that every collective agreement which is made in writing after the commencement of the Act shall be conclusively presumed to be intended by the parties to be a legally binding contract, unless there is a provision therein which states (however expressed) that the agreement (or part of it) is not intended to be legally enforceable. In other words, the Act makes a conclusive presumption concerning the intentions of the parties, which is capable of being rebutted by a written statement to the contrary. There are, however, a number of points to note. The new presumption only applies to written agreements made after the commencement of the Act. The legal affect of any pre-1971 agreements, and of any oral agreements made after 1971, must be determined by the pre-1971 law, which, as stated, is not certain. Indeed, the Industrial Relations Act implicitly assumes that pre-1971 collective agreements were capable of being legally enforceable, and makes special provision for some of these.   [242]

If an agreement was made between a trade union and an employers' association before the Act, then, as stated, the provisions of section 4 of the 1871 Act would apply. The repeal of that Act would mean that all such agreements were potentially legally enforceable. However, in such a case, if the agreement is broken after the Industrial Relations Act comes into force, the only legal remedy available to a complainant is an order from the NIRC determining the rights of the respective parties (section 105 (6)), not an award of compensation. Thus since a declaration was the only remedy for a breach of an agreement caught by the 1871 Act, the position has remained unchanged.   [243]

It is submitted, however, that in view of the new legalistic climate, and the need to have complete clarity on the subject, the NIRC will probably not follow the decision in *Ford Motor Co.* v. *A.U.E.F.W.* and one may hazard a guess that pre-1971 agreements will be held to be legally binding unless there is the clearest possible indication (not necessarily in writing) that the parties entered into the agreement with the intention that it should be "binding in honour only". This is particularly likely to happen if the NIRC should refer to the guiding principles in section 1, for subsection (1) (c) refers to "responsible and effective bodies", and a trade union and/or an employers' association will be acting with responsibility if it accepts onus of carrying out of an agreement backed by the due solemnity of the law. The point becomes relevant if one considers the nature of the agreements which are likely to be signed after the Act. In

[6] [1969] 2 Q.B. 303.

most cases, all that the parties agree to will be the "price list" clauses, namely, the terms and conditions which the parties are not going to carry out themselves, but which they are going to recommend to their members. (In practical terms, this means that the employers' association will circulate its membership with the new wage agreement; if the bargainer were an employer, bargaining on his own behalf, it is unlikely that, having agreed to pay a wage increase, he will then resile from it.) In so far as the parties themselves are not going to carry out this particular obligation, there is nothing to be legally enforced. The "contractual" clauses of a collective agreement generally relate to the procedure for settling disputes; most of these are already in existence, and it would be inconsistent if future (or new) agreements came under the statutory presumption concerning their legal effect, but existing agreements were held to be non-binding.
[244]

There are known to be in existence a number of pre-1971 agreements which are admitted to be legally enforceable, and the main trouble with the "no intention" theory is that it is used as a magic formula to try to find a means of escape from legal liability whenever one party to a collective agreement seeks to avoid a provision therein. Very few existing agreements have a "no intention" clause, and to seek the *actual* intentions of those who have already entered into agreements it may be necessary to invoke the services of a spiritualist rather than a lawyer. It becomes necessary, therefore, to "impute" intentions, by using the ficticious device of the "objective" test, which is even less satisfactory. It is submitted that the presumption of law, either by virtue of sections 34 and 35 of the Industrial Relations Act, or by virtue of common law rules (*Edwards* v. *Skyways, Ltd.,* [1964] 1 All E.R. 494), is that a commercial agreement is intended to be legally binding unless there is an express contrary intention, has greater merits than techniques which may involve necromancy or fictions. It must be further noted that although the Act applies the conclusive presumption to post-1971 written agreements, there is no particular reason why an oral agreement should not be equally legally binding, in the absence of strong evidence indicating the intentions of the parties. This is particularly so if the written and oral agreement are associated. For example, suppose a collective agreement to which the statutory presumption applies states that a trade union will not call a strike unless it gives the employer one month's notice. At the end of such period of notice, a trade union official orally promises that no strike will be called for a further period of one month. Provided all the other elements of a contract are present (consideration, etc.), there is no reason in law why this oral promise cannot be enforced.   **[245]**

The Act applies a similar presumption of intention to be legally bound to the written resolutions, decisions and awards of voluntary joint negotiating bodies, consisting of representatives of organisations of workers and representatives of employers or organisations of employers established by a collective agreement before or after the Act for the purpose of regulating the terms and conditions of employment of workers, or determining any matter for which a procedure agreement can provide (section 35). It is conclusively presumed that the parties represented on that joint body intend to authorise it to make a legally enforceable contract, and, so far as decisions, resolutions and awards are made after the Act, and are made in writing, and do not contain a provision stating (however expressed) that the decision is not intended to be legally enforceable, it will be conclusively presumed that there was an intention to create a legally enforceable contract on behalf of the constitutent bodies. This will apply, for example, to the decisions of joint negotiating councils, works committees, etc., on which there are representatives of organisations of workers and employers or employers' organisations. Plant bargaining clearly comes within the statutory presumption. The legal effect of such decisions made before the Act is still open to doubt, but if the agreement was made with the authority of the organisations concerned, then, assuming that *Ford Motor Co.* v. *A.U.E.F.W.* is wrong, they will be legally binding. It is possible, however, that the NIRC may take the view that in so far as an agreement consists of oral practices and understandings, some of these are not suitable for legal enforcement, as being too vague, and will confine such enforcement to all written agreements and such oral agreements as are capable of being enforced.   **[246]**

(b) *Non-existent or defective procedure agreements* (**sections 37-42**)
    A frequent cause of industrial friction has been the absence of a procedure agreement, or, where one has been in existence, it has shown itself to be defective in one or more ways. To remedy this, an application may now be made to the NIRC in respect of a particular unit of employment. The application may be made by: **[247]**

    (a) the Secretary of State; (b) the employer; (c) a trade union recognised as having negotiating rights in relation to that unit; or (d) where a procedure agreement is in existence, a trade union which is a party thereto, but which is not so recognised.   **[248]**

    The application will be made on the grounds that there is an absence of a procedure agreement, or that an existing one is unsuitable for settling disputes and grievances promptly and fairly, or that an existing agreement is flouted by constant resort to industrial action contrary to its terms or intentions.

Before the Secretary of State can make an application, he must first consult the relevant parties. Before the employer or trade union can make the application, they must first give notice to the Secretary of State of their intention to make it, and he will offer such advice and assistance as he may consider appropriate with a view to promoting an agreement, and, for this purpose, may refer any question relating to the matter to the CIR. The parties, however, may proceed with the application to the NIRC nonetheless.   [249]

If the NIRC thinks that the unit is suffering from any of these defects and, as a result, the development or maintenance of orderly industrial relations has been seriously impeded, or there has been substantial and repeated losses of working time in that unit, it can refer the matter to the CIR for examination, and ask for recommendations as to a remedy. The CIR will then examine the matter, and if they agree that the defect does exist but can be remedied by bringing new provisions into effect, or revising existing provisions, by alteration, deletion or addition, and that either the new or revised provisions ought to apply to a larger unit of employment than the one in the reference, they will after consultation with the employer and any trade union likely to be affected, formulate proposals as to that unit of employment. These proposals will be sent to the NIRC, and published as appropriate, in order to bring them to the attention of persons who would be affected. The latter persons have two weeks in which to apply to the NIRC for the matter to be re-considered, and on such application, the NIRC will either confirm the enlargement of the unit to which the new or revised provisions will relate, or direct that the scope remains unchanged. If no such application is made, the NIRC will confirm the extension made by the CIR.

                                                                                [250]

Having settled, if necessary, the size of the unit of employment, the CIR must now determine who are to be the parties to the reference. They will select the parties to any existing agreement which applies to that unit (or larger unit, as the case may be), and any other persons, being either employers, employers' associations or trade unions who would be appropriate parties to any new or revised procedure agreement. The CIR will then promote discussions with these parties with a view to obtaining their agreement on the new or revised proposals, which must be so formulated as to be capable of having effect as a legally binding agreement.   [251]

The CIR, however, if they are satisfied that the purpose for which the reference was made has been adequately fulfilled without continuing proceedings, may make a report to this effect to the NIRC, which may, on the application of any of the parties to the reference (i.e., the Secretary of State, the employer or trade union), withdraw the reference. Failing this, the CIR will report to the NIRC setting out the new or revised provisions they think are required, and which would have the effect of a legally binding agreement. If, as a result of its discussions with the parties, they have agreed to the acceptance of particular provisions, these will be included in the CIR's recommendations, but other provisions may be added by the CIR.   **[252]**

A copy of the report will be sent to the NIRC and to the parties to the reference. At any time within six months, any employer or trade union may apply to the NIRC for an order, which the NIRC will make unless it is satisfied that the order is not necessary for the purpose of securing the acceptance and observance of the provisions recommended in the report. The order will:

(a) define the unit of employment to which those provisions are to apply;

(b) specify the parties on whom they are to be binding; and

(c) direct that after a stated date, and so long as the order remains in force, those provisions shall have effect as a legally binding contract.

At any time thereafter, all the parties may jointly apply to the NIRC to have the order revoked, or varied, which the court will do. It will also entertain an application for revocation (but not variation) from one of the parties without the concurrence of the others, and if it thinks that the order is no longer necessary for the purpose of securing the observance of its provisions, the NIRC may revoke it. Before doing so, it may request the CIR to examine and report. Other than this, once the CIR have made their report to the NIRC, they will not entertain any further such application for two years relating to the same unit of employment on this issue unless it is satisfied that there are special reasons.   **[253]**

(c) *Unfair industrial practices* **(section 36)**

It will be an unfair industrial practice for any party to a legally binding collective agreement to break it or any legally binding part of such agreement: section 36 (1). It will also be an unfair industrial practice (section 36 (2)) for any party to such an agreement *made after the commencement of the Act* not to take all such steps as are reasonably practicable for the purpose of:

(a) preventing persons purporting to act on behalf of that party from taking any action contrary to an undertaking given in the agreement;

(b) preventing members of any organisation from taking any such action; and

(c) securing that any such action mentioned in (a) and (b) is not continued and does not recur.   [254]

This applies to agreements which have been arrived at voluntarily and to those which are the subject of an order from the NIRC (above). The remedy for such unfair industrial practices will be a complaint to the NIRC (and to no other court) under section 101, which may award an order on rights, the payment of compensation, and a desisting order, as appropriate. The compensation award will be subject to the limits imposed by section 117 (see para. [146], *ante*) if the action is against a trade union.   [255]

Section 36 (2) is bound to create a number of difficulties, particularly over the question as to what steps are reasonably practicable to prevent members of trade unions (or organisations of workers) from taking action in violation of a collective agreement. It is submitted that there are two separate problems. The first concerns the shop steward (or perhaps the local full time official) who calls a strike in breach of the agreement. Trade unions can deal with this matter by removing such power from the hands of the official or steward in question by the union rules, or alternatively, by providing that any strike must be sanctioned by a higher authority. Any strike thus called is a breach of those rules, rendering the person responsible to appropriate disciplinary action. As long as the official union policy in regard to an unofficial strike which is a breach of a collective agreement is one of opposition, and the union, through its officials, attempt to get the strikers back to work, it will have taken all reasonably practicable steps. (In so far as the rules of a union provide that all strikes are official, it is doubtful if such rules will get past the Registrar, but if they do they should be altered at once.) In practice this means that union officials will be doing no more than that which they have been doing for long before the Industrial Relations Act was passed. The second problem concerns the members. There are no other reasonably practicable steps for preventing individual members from acting in breach of the agreement, though it is possible that such conduct, if persisted in by a few ringleaders, may be grounds for expulsion, and a union which refuses to do this may find it has fallen short of the standards required by the Act. This is particularly so in those cases where an agency shop agreement or an approved closed shop agreement is in existence, for the complaining employer can argue that expulsion amounts to an effective deterrent, which is reasonably practicable. This may not prevent unofficial strikes from breaking out, but it will exonerate the union from liability! (It may be possible to fine or otherwise discipline a mass of members, though whether this is reasonably practicable must be a moot point.)   **[256]**

However, it must be remembered that the obligation in section 36 (2) only applies to those collective agreements made after the Act comes into force, and which are legally binding contracts. Collective agreements made before the Act comes into operation, whether legally binding or not, do not give rise to this obligation. The same is true of collective agreements made after the commencement of the Act which are not legally binding by virtue of a clause in writing excluding any intention on the part of the parties to be legally bound thereby. Nor does a trade union have any responsibility in respect of the actions of non-members, including those who pay contributions under an agency shop agreement.   **[257]**

(d) *Notification of procedure agreements* **(section 58)**

The Secretary of State is empowered to make regulations requiring employers of any description, or any particular employer:

(a) to inform him if he is a party to a procedure agreement, or has agreed to observe its terms if he is not a party thereto;

(b) to furnish him with a copy of a procedure agreement to which he is a party;

(c) if he is not a party to, but has agreed to observe, a procedure agreement, then either to furnish him with a copy or such particulars as are necessary to identify it;

(d) to inform him of the description and numbers of employees who are, or who are not, covered by the procedure agreement.
                    [258]

The regulations may exempt employers who provide this information in pursuance of a voluntary arrangement.   **[259]**

(e) *The normative effect of collective agreements*

In this respect, the law remains unchanged, and the following summary is included for the sake of completeness.   **[260]**

The terms of a collective agreement may be incorporated into the individual contract of employment in three ways:

(i) *Expressly.* This is done when the contract specifically makes reference to the "national agreement"[7] or "union conditions", etc., though the precise scope of these phrases has still to be defined. For example, it is possible to argue that "union rates of pay" is a narrower term that "union conditions", etc. Further, a notice served under the Contracts of Employment Act 1963 may refer to a document (Blue Book, etc.) which contains all the relevant terms and conditions of employment.[8]   **[261]**

(ii) *Impliedly.* Sometimes, it is possible to argue that the terms and

[7] *National Coal Board* v. *Galley,* [1958] 1 All E.R. 91.
[8] *Camden Exhibition & Display Ltd.* v. *Lynott,* [1966] Q.B. 555.

conditions laid down in a national or local agreement have been followed or observed for such a long time, or the circumstances were such that it was "obvious" to all concerned that they are to be regarded as part of the contract of employment—so obvious, in fact, that the parties did not make an express provision to this effect in the individual contract of employment.[9] In respect, it is possible that a trade union member is in a more favourable position than a non-unionist, for there is less scope for the implied incorporation of all the terms of a collective agreement in favour of the latter.[10] A collective agreement which is expressed to be not legally enforceable as between the parties may nonetheless become a legally binding part of the individual contract of employment if it is expressly or impliedly incorporated into that contract.   **[262]**

(iii) *Section* 8 *of the Terms and Conditions of Employment Act* 1959. A major problem surrounding the enforcement of the normative aspect of collective agreement has always been the non-federated employer who was not bound (necessarily) thereby. The procedure under section 8 is designed to enable either a trade unionist (through his trade union), or an employer (through his association) to force "the outsider" to comply with the minimum terms agreed upon by the "good" employer. The procedure is now as follows (see section 152 and 7th Schedule of the Industrial Relations Act); first a claim must be reported to the Secretary of State; only a trade union or employers' association registered under the Industrial Relations Act may do this. If he is satisfied that a collective agreement exists generally, or for the district or industry in question, and that the employers' association and the trade union(s) represent a substantial proportion of the workers and employers in that industry, and that a particular employer is not observing those terms in respect of a worker who should be covered by the agreement, he will try to settle the matter by discussion and/or concilliation. If this fails, he will refer the matter for settlement to the IAB. The Industrial Relations Act makes a minor amendment in the law by enabling claims to be brought under section 8 in respect of workers who come under Wage Councils. If the IAB find that the claim is well founded and that the employer in question is observing terms and conditions of employment which are less favourable than the recognised terms and conditions, the IAB may make an order requiring the employer to observe the recognised terms in respect of those employees, and any such award becomes an implied term of their contracts of employment. The award may be backdated, but not earlier than the time on which the employer was first informed that the claim was being made.   **[263]**

[9] *MacLea* v. *Essex Lines* (1933), 45 Lloyds L.R. 254.
[10] *London Passenger Board* v. *Muscrop,* [1942] 1 All E.R. 97.

CHAPTER FIVE

LEGAL REMEDIES

The central feature of the Industrial Relations Act is the legal remedies which are provided for wrongful acts. These may be placed into five categories: actions in tort, unfair industrial practices, remedies for breach of duty, criminal actions and residual liabilities.

[264]

A. ACTIONS IN TORT

Under the pre-1971 law there were four headings of tortious liability which could be invoked in trade disputes. These were:

(a) an action for inducing or procuring a breach of contract;
(b) conspiracy;
(c) intimidation; and
(d) malicious interference with trade, business or employment.

[265]

(a) *Inducing or procuring a breach of contract*

In *Lumley* v. *Gye*[1] an opera singer agreed to sing at a theatre owned by the plaintiff. The defendant, a rival impressario, induced her to break this contract and to sing for him instead. It was held that the plaintiff, as well as having a right against the singer by virtue of the contract with her, also had the right against the whole world not to have that contract interfered with without lawful justification. Thus the action for inducing a breach of contract was successful. So far as industrial relations are concerned, an employer has the right to his workers' services by virtue of the contract of employment which subsists between them, and anyone who calls those workers out on strike is inducing a breach of that contract. The Trade Disputes Act of 1906 recognised that trade unions needed protection against this particular tort, and an act "done in furtherance or contemplation of a trade dispute" was not to be actionable only on the grounds that it induced a breach of *contract of employment*. The Industrial Relations

---

[1] (1853), 2 E. & B. 216.

Act continues that protection by providing (section 132 (1)) that an act done by a person in contemplation or furtherance of an industrial dispute shall not be actionable in tort on the ground only:

> (a) that it induces another person to break a contract to which that other person is a party or prevents another person from performing such a contract . . .   **[266]**

This section is narrower than the 1906 section it replaces, in that the definition of an industrial dispute is narrower than the old "trade dispute". On the other hand, it is considerably wider, in that the 1906 Act only provided a defence in respect of inducing breaches of contracts of employment, whereas the Industrial Relations Act refers to all contracts. Further there is protection against a tort action brought in respect of preventing another person from performing a contract, which again is wider than the old provisions.

An "industrial dispute" means any dispute between one or more employers or organisations of employers and one or more workers or organisations of workers where the dispute relates wholly or mainly to:

> (a) the terms and conditions of employment, or the physical conditions in which any workers are required to work;
> (b) the engagement or non-engagement or termination or suspension of one or more workers;
> (c) the allocation of work as between workers or groups of workers;[2]
> (d) a procedure agreement, or any matter to which a procedure agreement can relate.

A dispute between a Minister of the Crown and one or more organisations of workers shall still be an industrial dispute within the meaning of the definition even though the Minister is not the employer of any of the workers to whom the dispute relates, if it refers to matters which are being considered by a joint body on which the Minister is represented, or in respect of which a settlement cannot take place without the exercise of a power conferred on that Minister. Thus a dispute on the Burnham Committee between the teachers side and the Minister will be an industrial dispute, even though the teachers are employed by, and are necessarily in dispute with, local authorities.   **[267]**

Tort immunities in respect of acts done in furtherance of contemplation of an industrial dispute are to be found in section 132

---

[2] Thus, a "who-does-what" dispute is within the definition of an industrial dispute.

(inducing a breach of contract, interfering with trade and conspiracy), and section 135 (picketing). It must be noted in particular, however, that an inter-union dispute is not an industrial dispute. Supposing two organisations of workers are in dispute about bargaining rights in a particular undertaking. The proper way to deal with the matter is to apply for a sole bargaining agency or joint negotiating panel (see Chapter 4), or for the employer to do so. If either organisation or worker calls a strike (not otherwise being an unfair industrial practice) tort liability may arise, based on an action for inducing a breach of contract (of employment), and section 132 will not afford a defence.[3] However, the Act does not prevent organisations of workers from settling inter-union disputes by any other available machinery, e.g., the Bridlington Agreement, or by using the machinery of the T.U.C. Legal liability arises when they involve others (usually employers) who are not really concerned in the dispute.   **[268]**

It is possible to defend an action based on inducing a breach of contract on the ground that there was justification for inducing the breach. Thus in *Brimelow* v. *Casson*,[4] the defendant induced some chorus girls to break their contract with the plaintiff. It was shown that the wages paid by the plaintiff were so low that the girls had to resort to prostitution in order to earn a living. The defendant, therefore, successfully raised the defence of justification. However, in *South Wales Miners Federation* v. *Glamorgan Coal Co.*,[5] a trade union called a strike in order to obtain an improvement in their wages. It was held that this did not amount to legal justification. Thus it is clear that this defence can only apply in unusual circumstances. Supposing an organisation of workers called a strike against working conditions which were manifestly unsafe and dangerous. It is submitted that justification would be a good answer to a tort action based on inducing a breach of contract, irrespective of any statutory defence. For the elements of the wrongful act of inducing a breach of contract, see para. **[308]**, *post.*   **[269]**

(b) *Conspiracy*

The tort of conspiracy is committed whenever two or more persons combine together to commit an unlawful act, or a lawful act by unlawful means. Thus in *Quinn* v. *Leathem*,[6] L was a butcher who employed non-union labour. The union called upon him to dismiss them, but he refused to do so. Instead, he offered to pay the arrears of their subscriptions if they were admitted to the union. This offer was refused. M supplied meat to L, and the union threatened to call a

---

[3] See *Stratford* v. *Lindley*, [1965] A.C. 269.   [4] [1924] 1 Ch. 302.
[5] [1905] A.C. 239.   [6] [1901] A.C. 495.

93

strike among M's employees unless he ceased to supply L. M complied with this request. It was held that the union had committed the tort of conspiracy. Their motive was not the legitimate one of advancing their trade union interest, but to cause harm to L and the non-unionists, and this turned their actions into an unlawful act.
[270]

The Industrial Relations Act provides (section 132 (3)) that an agreement or combination by two or more persons to do or procure to be done any act in contemplation or furtherance of an industrial dispute shall not be actionable in tort, if the act in question is one which, if done without such agreement or combination, would not be actionable in tort. In other words, one must look at the alleged act which is the subject of the conspiracy charge, and see if it would be actionable if done by an individual. If the answer is in the negative, no wrong is committed. Thus, if a group of workers, in furtherance of an industrial dispute, commit a trespass, then since their actions would be actionable if committed by one individual, the combined actions will amount to a tortious conspiracy. In *Allen* v. *Flood*,[7] the defendant called out certain workmen (without breaking their contracts of employment) on strike in order to procure the dismissal of some other workmen. It was held that no wrongful act was committed and that he was doing that which he was lawfully entitled to do. The difficulty with this case is that, although it is a House of Lords decision, that House is no longer bound by its own decisions, and it is thought that at some future date another House may not follow it. The result would be that a new tort, causing harm maliciously, may emerge, which may outflank the protection of the Industrial Relations Act on this point. For if the act in *Allen* v. *Flood* was held to be wrongful if done by an individual a fortiori it becomes actionable as a conspiracy.   **[271]**

Despite this, a further protection exists. If in any court proceedings based on conspiracy, section 132 (3) does not form a defence, the court shall stay the proceedings if it is satisfied that either of the conditions specified in section 131 (2) is fulfilled. These conditions are (1) that the act is one in respect of which proceedings under the Industrial Relations Act have been brought before the NIRC or an industrial tribunal, whether disposed of or not, or (2) that the act is one in respect of which (as being an unfair industrial practice or breach of duty imposed by the Act) proceedings could be brought before the NIRC or an Industrial Tribunal.   **[272]**

The result is now as follows. If the alleged wrongful act is an unfair industrial practice under the Industrial Relations Act, proceedings must be brought in the NIRC or Industrial Tribunal as

[7] [1898] A.C. 1.

the case may be, and no action in tort in the ordinary courts for conspiracy is possible. If however, no such unfair industrial practice has been committed, the old law is still applicable. Further, the NIRC has no jurisdiction to deal with tort actions, so the case must be brought in the ordinary courts. For example, *Quinn* v. *Leathem* concerns the right not to join an organisation of workers: an infringement of that right is an unfair industrial practice under section 5 (1), and this is now actionable as such, not in tort; section 33 (3) (a). On the other hand if the wrongful act concerns the further-ance of a personal grudge, the tort action may still subsist. Thus in *Huntley* v. *Thornton*,[8] the plaintiff was involved in a dispute with local trade union officials, who purported to expel him from the union. The expulsion was not upheld by the national executive committee of the union. Nonetheless, the local officials still regarded him as non-member, and took steps to ensure that he could not get a job. It was held that they were pursuing a personal grudge, not legitimate trade union activities and were liable for conspiracy. Thus, supposing a group of workers tried to prevent a person from obtaining employment by the threat of industrial action, and the reason was his membership or non-membership of a trade union or organisation of workers. As this would amount to an unfair industrial practice, the tort action in respect of conspiracy must be stayed. However, if the reason was related (say) to his political opinions, the tort action still subsists. If one person tried to prevent another from obtaining employment by the threat of industrial action which was not itself otherwise wrongful in such circumstances, the tort of maliciously interfering with another's trade, etc., may well be revived. A conspiracy does not exist if an organisation of workers is pursuing legitimate trade union interests,[9] though the list of what is, and what is not legitimate, is now considerably narrowed as a result of the Industrial Relations Act. Attempts to enforce a closed shop,[10] are now outlawed by section 7 (except for approved closed shop agreements); opposing a colour bar is legitimate,[11] but enforcing one would be an unfair industrial practice (section 149); striking for higher wages is a legitimate object (but not a strike called in breach of a collective agreement, section 36), while the threat of a strike unless a non-unionist is dismissed is an unfair industrial practice under section 5 (1).   [273]

---

[8] [1957] 1 All E.R. 234.
[9] *Crofter Hand Woven Harris Tweed* v. *Veitch*, [1942] A.C. 435.
[10] *Reynolds* v. *Shipping Federation*, [1924] 1 Ch. 28.
[11] *Scala Ballroom (Wolverhampton), Ltd.* v. *Ratcliffe*, [1958] 3 All E.R. 220.

(c) *Intimidation*

The tort of intimidation may be defined as a threat to do an unlawful act which causes damage to a person. This tort, thought to be "obscure and unfamiliar" was revised in the case of *Rookes* v. *Barnard*,[12] a case which more than any other sparked off the debate on the reform of industrial relations. Briefly, Rookes resigned from his trade union, and the three defendants informed his employers that there would be a strike if he was not dismissed. As the strike would have been in breach of contracts in respect of two of the defendants, it was held that they had threatened to do an unlawful act, i.e., threatened to break a contract of employment, and thus they were held liable for damages. This loophole in trade union law, which many saw as a threat to the right to strike, was plugged by the Trade Disputes Act of 1965, which is now repealed, but its provisions are re-enacted in the Industrial Relations Act. Section 132 (1) provides that "An act done by a person in contemplation or furtherance of an industrial dispute shall not be actionable in tort on the grounds only . . . (b) that it consists in his threatening that a contract (whether one to which he is party or not) will be broken or will be prevented from being performed, or that he will induce another person to break a contract to which that other person is a party or will prevent another person from performing such a contract". It will be noted that the person making the threat need not be a party to the contract himself; this meets the position of one of the defendants in *Rookes* v. *Barnard*, Silverthorne, who was a full time trade union official, and thus did not have a contract of employment with Rookes's employers to threaten to break.   **[274]**

(d) *Malicious interference with trade, business or employment*

It has been suggested in some recent cases that new tort liabilities may arise, including the tort of maliciously interfering with the trade, business or employment of another. Malicious here means without lawful motive or justification. Also under this heading comes the possible tort action of wrongfully interfering with future contracts. It is not possible to explore these ideas further, and it is to be hoped that the question remains academic. It should be noted that section 132 (2) of the Industrial Relations Act revives the second limb of section 3 of the 1906 Act by providing than for the avoidance of doubt an act done by a person in contemplation or furtherance of an industrial dispute shall not be actionable in tort on the ground only that it is an interference with the trade, business or employment of another person, or with the right of another person to dispose of his capital or his labour as he wills.   **[275]**

[12] [1964] A.C. 1129.

Finally, it must be noted that the Industrial Relations Act has repealed the whole of the Trade Disputes Act 1906; this means that the former complete immunity in respect of actions in tort which was possessed by trade unions by virtue of section 4 of that Act no longer exists. An action in tort against a trade union or any other organisation of workers may now be brought in defamation, negligence, nuisance, etc., as it could be brought against any other person. The only immunities possessed by a trade union or organisation of workers are those expressed in the statute, namely, so far as actions in contemplation of an industrial dispute are concerned, the protections given in sections 132 and 134 to any person, and the immunity conferred on trade unions and their officials by virtue of sections 96 and 97 in respect of an unfair industrial practice[12a].   **[276]**

Thus it will be seen that all the tort actions of the previous law still subsist (but see discussion of section 147 in Chapter 8), together with the various statutory defences which existed, with slight modifications. The point of the Industrial Relations Act, however, is to prevent tort actions being brought in respect of industrial disputes, and providing instead a set of specified remedies in respect of unfair industrial practices. Thus the ordinary courts are directed (section 131) that where any proceedings in tort are brought against any person in respect of an act done by him or on his behalf, the court may stay the proceedings if either of two conditions is satisfied. These are (a) that the act is one in respect of which proceedings under the Industrial Relations Act have been brought before the NIRC or an Industrial Tribunal, whether those proceedings have been disposed of or not, or (b) that the act is one in respect of which proceedings could be brought before the NIRC or an Industrial Tribunal on the ground that the act complained of was an unfair industrial practice or breach of duty under the Industrial Relations Act. The same rule applies to interlocutory actions.   **[277]**

It will be noted that the courts *may* stay the proceedings; this is to prevent the situation arising where a plaintiff has a good case, but is in danger of falling between the two stools if there is some doubt as to the court in which proceedings should be brought. The result is that if a complaint amounts to an allegation of an unfair industrial practice, proceedings should be brought in the NIRC or Industrial Tribunal, as the case may be. If it is a tort action simpliciter, the case will go to the ordinary courts. Thus, to take an example, supposing there was a threat to slash the tyres of a non-unionist. This would amount to an act of intimidation, and is actionable as a tort. If, however, the threat was to slash the tyres of the employer unless he

---

[12a] For the protection of section 147, see Chapter 8.

97

dismissed a non-unionist, this would be an unfair industrial practice by virtue of section 33 (3) (a), and is actionable in the NIRC only.
[278]

B. UNFAIR INDUSTRIAL PRACTICES

The Industrial Relations Act contains a long list of unfair industrial practices, some of which may be committed by a trade union or an organisation of workers, or by individual workers, individuals who lead strike action (but never by the actual strikers as such), and some of which may be committed by an employer or an organisation of employers. We will examine each act in turn.
[279]

(a) *Unfair industrial practices by trade unions, organisations of workers and workers*

If any person (including any organisation, etc.) does any of the following acts, namely:

(a) calling, organising, procuring or financing a strike, or threatening to do so; or

(b) organising, procuring or financing irregular industrial action short of a strike, or threatening to do so,[13]

he may, in any of the circumstances outlined below, be guilty of committing an unfair industrial practice. He will not be so guilty if he is not caught by these provisions, though, of course, tort or other liability may exist in appropriate cases. Nor is he guilty if he does something other than the above acts except where such contingency is provided for. In other words, not all strikes, etc., are wrongful, and not all wrongful acts are strikes, etc.
[280]

A strike is defined as a concerted stoppage of work by a group of workers in contemplation of furtherance of an industrial dispute, whether they are parties to the dispute or not, whether the stoppage is or is not in breach of their terms and conditions of employment, and whether it is carried out during, or on the termination of, their employment. One person, therefore, does not go on strike. Irregular industrial action short of a strike means any concerted course of conduct (other than a strike) which, in contemplation or furtherance of an industrial dispute:

(a) is carried on by a group of workers with the intention of preventing, reducing, or otherwise interfering with the production of goods or the provisions of services; *and*

---

[13] Thus, a person who "calls" for irregular industrial action commits no wrongful act under this heading, providing he does not "organise, procure or finance" it. However, there may be liability in respect of inducing a breach of contract, for which see para. [306], *post.*

(b) in the case of some or all of them, is carried on in breach of their contracts of employment or (where they are not employees) in breach of their terms and conditions of service.

Thus, a go-slow, being a breach of contract of employment, would be irregular industrial action short of a strike. A work-to-rule, on the other hand, is the literal performance of the contract of employment, and only becomes irregular industrial action if some of the workers go beyond the literal performance of their contract, by, for example, working to non-existent rules. The intention here is to throw the onus of observance on to those who organise the work-to-rule to ensure that it goes no further than the rules permit. A refusal to work overtime may amount to irregular industrial action if the workers are bound by their contracts of employment to work a certain amount of overtime, otherwise it is not. A refusal to perform certain duties, being a breach of the contract of employment, will be irregular industrial action, as will a refusal to work with certain workers where this would prevent the normal employment functions from being carried on.   [281]

In so far as "sending a person to Coventry" does not interfere with the production of goods or the provision of services, it does not amount to irregular industrial action.   [282]

The following unfair industrial practices arise out of strike action or irregular industrial actions short of a strike, or threats to do so:

(i) Knowingly to induce or attempt to induce an employer *not* to perform his duty to enter into an agency shop agreement (or not to perform his duty to carry out that agreement so long as it remains in force) after a ballot held under the provisions of the Act has shown that the requisite majority of workers were in favour of that agreement: section 13 (2).   [283]

Supposing a group of workers object to paying the appropriate contribution to a trade union which has obtained an agency shop as a result of a successful ballot. Their remedy is to apply for a discontinuance of that agreement after two years, not to take strike or other such action.   [284]

(ii) Knowingly to induce or attempt to induce an employer to enter into an agency shop agreement *after* an application has been made to the NIRC for the matter to be considered under section 11: section 16 (2) (a). However, if a ballot has been held which has proved in favour of the agency shop, it is not an unfair industrial practice to strike, etc., in order to enforce that agency shop on an unwilling employer: section 16 (2) (a).   [285]

(iii) Knowingly to induce or attempt to induce an employer to refrain from making an application to the NIRC under section 11 concerning an agency shop: section 16 (2) (b). This may arise where, for example, an employer objects to an agency shop agreement, and the trade union is threatening to strike unless he concedes one. If the union does not wish to take the matter to the NIRC, the employer can in order to ascertain the wishes of his employees, and it will be an unfair industrial practice to attempt to stop him by strike or other such action. **[286]**

(iv) Knowingly to induce an employer, or person acting on his behalf, to take any action which would be an unfair industrial practice on the part of the employer by virtue of section 5 (2) or section 22 (1): section 33 (3) (a). Since it is an unfair industrial practice for an employer to deter a workman from exercising the rights to join a union or not to join an organisation of workers, or for the employer to dismiss, penalise or otherwise discriminate against a worker, by reason of his exercising his rights, or to refuse to employ him on the grounds of his non-membership of an organisation of workers (except in agency shop or approved closed shop situation) then it is also an unfair industrial practice for any one knowingly to induce an employer to do any of these things. Thus, for example, a worker has the right not to join an organisation of workers in a non-agency shop situation. To dismiss him because of his non-unionism, is an unfair industrial practice committed by the employer. A strike to bring about that dismissal, or to induce the employer to dismiss him, is equally an unfair industrial practice and this is so whether or not the strike achieves its objective. A threat to strike is equally actionable, and therefore, in a *Rookes* v. *Barnard* situation, Rookes would now have an action against the defendants even if he were not dismissed. Should the employer dismiss him, the latter may be able to obtain some contributions from those concerned (see section 119). Similarly, it will equally be an unfair industrial practice knowingly to induce an employer to dismiss a worker contrary to section 22 (1) (right not to be unfairly dismissed). This may arise, for example, if workers tried to obtain a person's dismissal because they wished to uphold a colour bar. **[287]**

(v) Knowingly to induce an employer to enter into a closed shop agreement which would be void by section 7 (1) (but not an approved closed shop agreement) or to comply with a provision which would be void by that section. Thus, any strike to enforce a closed shop (other than an approved closed shop) is an unfair industrial practice: section 33 (3) (b). **[288]**

(vi) Knowingly to induce an employer to comply with a provision which the NIRC has declared to be void under section 7 (3). If a worker finds he is unable to obtain employment because an employer has a closed shop agreement which has not been approved, he may apply to the NIRC. If the court finds that a closed shop agreement exists (however expressed, and whether it purports to have that effect or not), that the refusal of the employer to engage the worker was wholly or partly attributable to a provision in that agreement and that this constitutes a substantial derogation of his rights under section 5 (1), the NIRC shall make an order declaring that provision to be void. Therefore an "informal" closed shop arrangement is not possible under the Act: section 33 (3) (c).   **[289]**

(vii) Knowingly to induce an employer or an employers' association to join in making an application for an approved closed shop agreement. If an employer wishes to have an approved closed shop agreement applicable to him, then he, and the union, may make a joint application. Such application must, however, be voluntary, and a strike to compel the employer to join in the application is an unfair industrial practice: section 33 (3) (d). A strike to compel an unregistered organisation of employers to join in such an application appears to be perfectly lawful.   **[290]**

(viii) Strikes or irregular industrial action while matters relating to the issue of the recognition of a sole bargaining agent are pending. Once a trade union, or an employer, either separately or jointly wish to make an application under section 45, they must first give notice of the proposal to the Secretary of State. Having done so, any question which would be a matter proposed to be referred by virtue of an application made in pursuance of that notice, or is so referred, or which is included in a reference by virtue of section 47, becomes a pending matter.   **[291]**

Where the notice of a proposal is made to the Secretary of State the matter remains pending until the time certified by the Secretary of State to be:

(1) The date on which agreement was reached on the matters to which the proposed application relates; or

(2) the date on which it became apparent that no such agreement was likely to be reached without an application to the NIRC. It would appear that a reference *by* the Secretary of State himself does not give rise to a pending matter, and the provisions to that extent do not apply to that case. Once the application is made to the NIRC, the matter *will* remain pending until:

(a) the NIRC decides not to refer the question to the CIR; or
(b) the reference to the CIR on that application is withdrawn; or
(c) the expiration of six months from the date when the CIR reports to the NIRC.

Any strike or irregular industrial action (or threat of such action) in furtherance of the dispute in question becomes an unfair industrial practice: section 54 (4).   **[292]**

(ix) When an order from the NIRC under section 48 is in force it will be an unfair industrial practice knowingly to induce an employer to carry on any collective bargaining with an organisation of workers which has not been designated as the bargaining agent by that order, or knowingly to induce the employer not to take such action by way of collective bargaining which might reasonably be expected to be taken by an employer ready and willing to carry on such bargaining. In other words, once the NIRC has designated the bargaining agent, the field is closed to all others until such time as the NIRC order is revoked: section 55 (3) (see para. **[199]**, *ante*).   **[293]**

(x) Knowingly to induce an employer to recognise as sole bargaining agency any organisation of workers which was not recommended in a CIR report for recognition under section 48. This, however, only applies to the period of two years from the time when the report is sent to the NIRC by the CIR, and is applicable to those cases where no NIRC order was obtained. It is equally an unfair industrial practice knowingly to induce or attempt to induce the employer to carry on any collective bargaining with any organisation of workers which was not so recognised for recognition in that report: section 55 (4).   **[294]**

(xi) Knowingly to induce an employer not to comply with an order from the NIRC directing the employer to cease to recognise a trade union as the sole bargaining agent, and not to recognise it as the sole bargaining agent for two years from the date of the ballot held on the question of the discontinuance of the sole bargaining agency under section 53: section 55 (5).   **[295]**

(xii) In contemplation or furtherance of an industrial dispute, to strike or take any irregular industrial action if the principal purpose is to further any action taken by him or any other person which is an unfair industrial practice: section 97. But any action taken (or threatened) by a trade union or an employers' association for the purpose of furthering any action taken by officials or members, and which consists only of an unfair industrial practice by virtue of section 96 (inducing breach of contract, see below) will not amount to an unfair industrial practice.   **[296]**

Section 97 may be illustrated as follows. If a group of workers go on unofficial strike (say, for higher pay), the only wrongful act would be committed by the leaders, who, if not protected by section 96 because they were acting within the scope of their authority on behalf of a trade union, would be liable for inducing a breach of contract. If the trade union now make the strike official, although it is furthering an unfair industrial practice, it will not incur liability under section 97. All other strikes called in support of action which is already an unfair industrial practice will be unfair by virtue of section 97. Thus, calling a sympathetic strike would come within the provision, as will an unregistered organisation of workers which gives official support to any unofficial and unconstitutional strike. But this will be so only if it can be shown that an unfair industrial practice has been committed by some-one. If a group of workers come out on strike leaderless (i.e. there is no-one inducing a breach of their contracts of employment), the actual strikers may be breaking their contracts (for which they can be sued, etc.) but no unfair industrial practice is being committed at this stage, and further action in support will not attract liability under section 97.

[297]

If an organisation of workers calls a strike which is an unfair industrial practice other than by virtue of section 96, sympathisers who contribute to a strike fund for the benefit of *the strikers* are not furthering an unfair industrial practice, though they may be doing so if they contribute to a strike fund for the benefit of the union (even though this is distributed to the actual strikers) for this may amount to the "financing" of the strike.

[298]

(xiii) To strike or take other irregular industrial action in contemplation or furtherance of an industrial dispute if:

(a) he knows or has reasonable grounds for believing that another person has entered into a contract (not being a contract of employment) with a party to that industrial dispute; and

(b) his purpose in taking those steps is to induce that other person to break that contract or prevent him from performing it; and

(c) that other person is an extraneous party in relation to that dispute: section 98.

So if a trade union is in dispute with an employer, a strike designed to cut off supplies from a third party to that employer would come within this provision,[14] if the union knew or had reasonable grounds for believing that a contract to deliver those supplies was in existence between the employer and the third party.[15] A third party is an extraneous party to the dispute if he is not a party to the dispute and has not, in contemplation or furtherance of that dispute, taken any action in material support of a party to the dispute. The fact that the third party is an associated employer to the employer engaged in the

[14] *Torquay Hotel Co. Ltd.* v. *Cousins*, [1962] 2 Ch. 106.
[15] *Emerald Construction Ltd.* v. *Lowthian*, [1966] 1 All E.R. 1013.

dispute, or that he is a member of an organisation of employers of which the employer in dispute is also a member, or that he has contributed to a fund which is available for distribution in respect of losses incurred in consequence of industrial disputes, and the contribution was made without specific reference to the dispute in question, or that he supplies or has agreed to supply goods or services to a party in dispute in pursuance of a contract entered into before the industrial dispute began, does not mean that the third party has taken any action in material support of the dispute.   [299]

It will be noted that no. (xii) and no. (xiii), above, and no. (xvii) below, specify certain unfair industrial practices which may be committed in contemplation or furtherance of an industrial dispute. It follows, therefore, that if there is no such industrial dispute, no unfair industrial practice is committed. However, the result may well be the revival of tort liability. Supposing a trade union calls a strike of dockers in order to prevent the loading of armaments on to a ship which is destined for a country whose policies and politics are abhorrent to the trade union. Since this is not an industrial dispute, there is no unfair industrial practice (assuming there is no such liability under any other heading). Equally the protection of section 132 (above) will not be available. We must fall back, therefore, on the common law rules relating to inducing breach of contract (i.e., the contract of employment between the dockers and the employers) procuring a breach of contract (e.g., between the employers and the shipping company), conspiracy (since the trade union was not defending any legitimate interests), and so forth (but see Chapter 8).   [300]

The following unfair industrial practices may be committed by strike action, irregular industrial action, *or by other means.*   [301]

(xiv) To break any legally enforceable collective agreement, or any legally enforceable part of an agreement. This might be done by calling a strike in breach of the procedure, or by the non-observance of any of its terms. For example, a trade union which refuses to take a dispute to arbitration in accordance with the terms of the agreement will be committing an unfair industrial practice: section 36 (1).
          [302]

(xv) In respect of legally binding agreements made after the Act came into force, not to take all such steps as are reasonably practical for the purpose of:

(a) preventing persons acting or purporting to act on behalf of a party to a legally enforceable agreement from taking any action contrary to an undertaking given by that party and contained in a collective agreement; or

(b) preventing any member of an organisation of workers from taking such action; or

(c) if such action has been taken, of securing that the action is not continued and that further such action does not recur: section 36 (2).

For this purpose, action will be regarded as being taken contrary to the undertaking if it is action which, if taken by the contracting party, would have been a breach of an undertaking given by that party, or it consists of doing something which was not to be done, or not doing something which was to be done. Supposing a collective agreement provides that all disputes shall be dealt with through a specified procedure. If a shop steward of a trade union refuses so to process a particular dispute, the union must immediately repudiate his action in order to avoid liability under this section.   **[303]**

Thus an organisation of workers would be liable if it failed to prevent a branch official or other person who had the power to call an official strike (e.g., a shop steward) from taking such action in breach of a legally binding agreement. It is not easy to see what steps an organisation of workers could take to prevent (b), except to try to dissuade such action. For example, if union members were threatening an unofficial strike in breach of an agreement, it would be reasonably practicable for the union to send its officials down to try to dissuade or prevent the strikers from going ahead. It should also refuse to give any assistance, material or otherwise, to the strikers, and it might be liable if it failed to remove strike leaders from positions of authority in order to prevent further outbreaks under (c). A trade union, however, has no responsibility for the actions of non-members, including workers who make an appropriate contribution under an agency shop agreement.   **[304]**

(xvi) To take or threaten to take any action against any member of an organisation of workers or any other person in contravention of the principles set out in section 65. These are the guiding principles which govern the conduct of such organisations in respect of their members, and admission to the organisation: section 66.   **[305]**

(xvii) In contemplation or furtherance of a trade dispute, knowingly to induce or threaten to induce any person to break a contract to which that other person is a party, unless the person so inducing is:

(a) a trade union; or

(b) does so within the scope of his authority on behalf of a trade union: section 96.

The term "contract" however, does not include a legally binding

105

collective agreement of part thereof (nor does it include an agreement made enforceable by section 41).   **[306]**

It cannot be an unfair industrial practice knowingly to induce the breach of a collective agreement which is not legally binding, for that is not a "contract", and therefore no question of inducing a breach of contract arises. It is not, therefore, an unfair industrial practice knowingly to induce or threaten to induce the breach of a collective agreement, although it will be an unfair industrial practice to *break* the agreement (see (xiv) above) or to further the breach of such agreement (see (xii) above). However, the term "contract" does include the normative terms of a collective agreement (whether legally binding or not) which have been incorporated expressly or impliedly into the individual contracts of employment, and it will be an unfair industrial practice knowingly to induce a breach of these contracts unless it is done by a trade union or official acting in the course of his authority.   **[307]**

Suppose a trade union or official calls a strike which is not in breach of an agreement or otherwise wrongful. By doing so, he may (a) induce a breach of the contracts of employment which exists between the workers and the employers, and (b) may induce a breach of a contract to supply goods made between the employer and a third party. No legal liability exists, and the strike is not actionable at the suit of the employer. But since only registered trade unions and their officials are protected by the section, it will be an unfair industrial practice for an unregistered organisation of workers to induce the breach of any contract, be it a commercial contract or contract of employment (except a legally binding collective agreement). Further, since it is an unfair industrial practice to utilise the method of the secondary strike against extraneous parties (see (xiii) above), inducing breaches of commercial contract will generally attract liability to all unions, registered or not, if the action is directed against the third party. It seems, therefore, that an unregistered organisation of workers can hardly call a strike without falling foul of the law, for whether a no-strike clause is incorporated into the workers individual contracts of employment by the individual workers or not, a strike is normally a breach of contract of employment by the individual workers, and the unregistered organisation of workers will be liable for inducing a breach of that contract.[16] A trade union, on the other hand, may induce the breach of any contract in contemplation or furtherance of an industrial dispute provided no other heading of legal liability exists.   **[308]**

[16] See, however, Chapter 8.

The precise limits of section 96 were the subject of considerable discussion, while the Act was being passed. In particular, it was feared that journalists or other commentators may find themselves liable under its provisions. The wrongful act of inducing breach of contract has five elements, all of which must be present. These are (1) a knowledge of the existence of the contract, (2) an intention to induce the breach, (3) the breach taking place, (4) the breach must be a result of the inducement, and (5) damage. A journalist who merely reports the facts of an industrial dispute does not induce a breach of it, and a general exhortation to strike may not be sufficient "knowledge" of the existence of any particular contract.[17] On the other hand, precise knowledge of the terms of a contract is not required. To induce means to provide reasons, but the courts have not found it easy to distinguish between that and "mere advice". A person induces if he provides the reasons with the intention that they should be acted upon; a person advises if he provides the reasons, and leaves it to the recipient to decide for himself whether or not to act thereon. Somewhere between these two concepts lies a narrow path along which officials of organisations of workers and others must tread with great care.   [309]

(b) *Unfair industrial practices committed by employers or organisations of employers*

Employers (or their organisations) can commit unfair industrial practices in a number of ways. The first is by instituting, carrying on, organising, procuring or financing a lock-out or by threatening to do so. The term "lock-out" means action which, in contemplation or furtherance of an industrial dispute, is taken by one or more employers, whether parties to the dispute or not, and which consists of the exclusion of workers from one or more factories, offices, or other places of employment or of the suspension of work in one or more such places, or of the collective, simultaneous or otherwise connected termination or suspension of employment of a group of workers. In this connection, the following unfair industrial practices arise.
                                    [310]

(i) Knowingly to induce or attempt to induce a trade union or joint negotiating panel or any other person to refrain from making any application under section 11 (application to the NIRC for an agency shop agreement) or section 14 (application to the NIRC for the discontinuance of an agency shop agreement): section 16.   [311]

(ii) To institute, etc., a lock-out while matters relating to the issue of the recognition of a sole bargaining agency are pending. In the

[17] This may amount to an indirect inducement (*Thomson* v. *Deakin*, [1952] Ch. 646) which is actionable if unlawful or wrongful means are used.

same circumstances as outlined above (unfair industrial practices committed by organisations of workers (xiii)), any employer directly concerned in the dispute relating to any question, commencing with a proposal made to the Secretary of State, through to six months from the time when the CIR issues its report, must refrain from taking lock-out measures: section 54 (4).   **[312]**

(iii) Knowingly to induce or attempt to induce any person to refrain from making an application in respect of recognition as a sole bargaining agent, or an application for the withdrawal of such recognition: section 55 (8).   **[313]**

(iv) To institute a lock-out, etc., if the purpose is to further another person in doing, in contemplation or furtherance of an industrial dispute anything which would be an unfair industrial practice by that person: section 97 (see paras. **[296] – [298]**, *ante*).   **[314]**

(v) To institute a lock-out, etc., in contemplation or furtherance of a trade dispute by way of action against extraneous parties (see unfair industrial practices by organisation of workers (xiii): section 98.   **[315]**

Other unfair industrial practices which may be committed by an employer or an organisation of employers (as the case may be) by a lock-out or any other means are: **[316]**

(vi) In contemplation of furtherance of a trade dispute, knowingly to induce or threaten to induce any person to break a contract to which that other person is a party, unless the person so inducing is: (a) an employers' association; or (b) does so within the scope of his authority; on behalf of an employers' association. This does not apply if the contract, the breach of which was so induced was a collective agreement (or an agreement made legally enforceable by section 41), but it does apply to the normative terms of a collective agreement which are incorporated expressly or impliedly into any contract of employment: section 96.   **[317]**

(vii) To prevent or deter a worker from exercising his rights to join a trade union, or not to join a trade union or other organisation of workers, or, where the worker is a member of a trade union to prevent or deter him from taking part in the activities of the union at an appropriate time, or seeking appointment or election as an official, and holding such office: section 5 (2) (a). However the employer does not deter or prevent a worker from exercising his right not to join a trade union or other organisation of workers by reason only that he seeks to encourage the worker to join a trade union which the employer recognises as having negotiating rights in respect of that worker: section 5 (3).   **[318]**

(viii) To dismiss, penalise or otherwise discriminate against a worker by reason of his exercising any of the right mentioned in (vii): section 5 (2) (b). However, it is not an unfair industrial practice to dismiss, penalise or otherwise discriminate against a worker if there is an agency shop agreement in force, or an approved closed shop agreement, and the worker has refused to join the union, or to pay an appropriate contribution to it, or to a charity, as the case may be: section 6 (2) (a).   [319]

(ix) To refuse to engage a worker on the grounds that, at the time when he applied for employment, he was a member of a trade union, or that he was not a member of an organisation of workers: section 5 (2) (c). This does not apply to those situations where an agency shop agreement is in force and the worker has refused to agree to join the union, or to pay an appropriate contribution to it, or to a charity. Nor is it an unfair industrial practice where an approved closed shop agreement is in force to refuse to engage a worker to whom the agreement applied or to dismiss, penalise or otherwise discriminate against him, on the grounds that he is not and has refused to be a member of the trade union: section 17 (5).   [320]

(x) To dismiss an employee unfairly: section 22 (1).   [321]

(xi) To break any legally enforceable collective agreement or any legally enforceable part of any such agreement: section 36 (1). If an employer agrees with a trade union to pay an increase in wages to all workers in his factory, and the agreement is legally enforceable, a failure by the employer to pay that increase would constitute a breach of that agreement.   [322]

(xiii) In respect of legally binding collective agreement, which are made after the commencement of the Act, not to take such steps as are reasonably practicable for the purpose:

(a) of preventing persons acting or purporting to act on behalf of a party to a legally enforceable agreement from taking action contrary to an undertaking given in the agreement;

(b) of preventing members of an organisation from taking such action;

(c) if such action has been taken as mentioned in (1) and (2); of securing that the action is not continued, and that further such action does not recur: section 36 (2).   [323]

In respect of (a) it could be argued that this would apply to a foreman or manager who acted against the terms of an agreement made with a trade union relating, for example, to production matters. (b) and (c) have more relevance to the obligations of an organisation of employers to ensure that its members observe the terms and conditions laid down in agreements with unions (except that a legally binding agreement can only be made with an employers' association by virtue of section 39). In a federated agreement, made between an organisation of employers and an organisation of workers, the employers' organisation is now obliged by virtue of section 36 (2) (b) and (c) to ensure that all its members comply with the agreement.   [324]

(xiii) If the NIRC makes an order under section 50 requiring an employer to recognise a trade union or joint negotiating panel as a sole bargaining agent, it will be an unfair industrial practice for him to bargain with any other organisation of workers, or not to take such action with a view to carrying on collective bargaining with that trade union as might reasonably be expected to be taken by an employer ready and willing to carry on such bargaining: section 55 (1). It will not, however, be an unfair industrial practice for him to bargain with a trade union represented on a joint negotiating panel which has been so recognised, if he does so in pursuance of an agreement whereby the panel has consented to his carrying on such bargaining. In other words, if a joint negotiating panel has obtained recognition rights, the employer may enter into separate negotiations with a single trade union on that panel, provided the panel agree to do this (see para. [198], *ante*).   [325]

(xiv) To take or threaten to take any action against any member of an organisation of employers or any other person in contravention of the principles referred to in section 69. These are the guiding principles which govern the conduct of the organisation in respect of its members, and admissions, and are the same principles as are applicable to organisations of workers: section 70.   [326]

C. BREACHES OF DUTY

The Industrial Relations Act imposes three separate duties on employers which must be observed, but which do not give rise to unfair industrial practices if he fails to carry them out.   [327]

(i) If, after a ballot, a majority of workers eligible to vote have voted in favour of an agency shop agreement, it shall be the duty of the employer to take all such action as is requisite on his part for the purpose of:

    (a) entering into an agency shop agreement in respect of the description of workers comprised in the ballot; and

    (b) after such agreement has been made, of carrying it out so long as it remains in force: section 13 (1). If the employer fails to do so, a complaint may be presented to the NIRC under section 102, which, if it finds to be well-founded, and if it considers it would be just and equitable to do so, may make one of the following orders:

(i) An order determining the rights of the trade union and of the employer in relation to the matters to which the complaint relates;

(ii) an order directing the employer to take such action in the fulfilment of the duty as, in the opinion of the court it would be within the power of the employer to take and is action which in the circumstances he ought to be required to take.   [328]

(ii) It shall be the duty of employers to disclose to trade union representatives for the purposes of all stages of collective bargaining all such information relating to his undertaking as is in the possession of the employer and is both:

(a) information without which the trade union representative would be to a material extent impeded in carrying on collective bargaining; and

(b) information which it would be in accordance with good industrial relations practice that the employer should disclose to them for the purpose of collective bargaining: section 56. In this connection regard may be had to the Code of Practice for the time being in force so far as is applicable, but not so as to exclude any other evidence as to what that practice is. The employer, however, need not disclose information:

(i) the disclosure of which would be contrary to the interests of national security;

(ii) which he could not disclose without contravening a prohibition imposed by statute (e.g., the Official Secrets Act);

(iii) which has been disclosed to him in confidence;

(iv) which related specifically to an individual, unless the disclosure could not reasonably be expected to be seriously prejudicial to him and he has consented to the disclosure;

(v) the disclosure of which would be seriously prejudicial to the interest of the employer's undertaking for reasons other than its effect on collective bargaining;

(vi) any information obtained by the employer for the purpose of bringing, prosecuting or defending any legal proceedings.   [329]

If an employer fails in his duty to make such disclosures, a complaint can be presented to the NIRC, which may provide either

111

of the remedies specified above under section 102. In addition, however, the NIRC may authorise the presentation of a claim to the IAB under section 126.　　　　　　　　　　　　　　　　**[330]**

(iii) In every undertaking where there are more than 350 persons employed on any date within a financial year, it shall be the duty of the employer to issue statements (relating to that financial year, and issued not less than six months after the end of that period), in writing, containing all such information as may be required in accordance with regulations issued by the Secretary of State. The statement must be issued to all persons employed in the undertaking on the date of its issue, except

  (a) persons who are employed for less than 21 hours per week;
  (b) persons who have been employed in the undertaking for less than 13 weeks;
  (c) persons who normally work outside Great Britain.

The Secretary of State may make exemptions from this duty, and has also the power to change the requirement that the duty applies in undertakings which employ more than 350 persons to a duty in respect of undertakings which have a smaller or larger number of employees: section 57. He may make regulations prescribing that the information contained in the statement shall extend to subsidiary or associated companies.　　　　　　　　　　　　　　　　**[331]**

Any person employed in the undertaking may make a complaint to the Industrial Tribunal alleging that the employer is required to fulfil this duty, and has failed to do so. The Industrial Tribunal may make an order determining the rights of the complainant and the employer to whom the complaint relates. It can also extend the time during which the duty may be fulfilled for a further period. If, despite this, the employer fails to carry out his duty to provide the statement, the complainant can make a further complaint to the NIRC. If it finds that the grounds for the complaint are well-founded, and considers that it would be just and equitable to do, the NIRC may make an order directing the employer before the end of such period as may be specified, to issue to the complainant a statement containing such information as the court thinks appropriate, having regard to the rights determined by the order of the Industrial Tribunal: section 110.　　　　　　　　**[332]**

D. CRIMINAL LIABILITIES

The Industrial Relations Act contains a number of criminal actions for which minor penalties are prescribed.　　　　　**[333]**

(i) By section 58, the Secretary of State may make regulations requiring an employer to notify him of procedural agreements, in cases where the employer is either a party to that agreement, or has agreed to observe it. (a) By section 59, any person who does not comply with those regulations within the specified period shall be guilty of an offence. (b) Further, any person who is required to furnish information by those regulations, and who makes a statement which he knows to be false in a material particular, or recklessly makes such a false statement, or, where he is required to furnish a copy of a procedure agreement, produces a copy which to his knowledge is not an accurate or complete copy, is guilty of an offence.

Under (a) the maximum penalty on summary conviction is £100, under (b) the maximum penalty is £400.   **[334]**

(ii) By section 87, a trade union and an employers' association shall keep proper accounting records, and establish and maintain satisfactory financial control. By section 88, every trade union and employers' association shall submit an annual return to the Registrar, appoint auditors, and publish an annual report for its members. The 5th Schedule contains a long list of the relevant rules for these purposes. By section 89 every trade union and employers' association shall inform the Registrar of any change in its rules, officers and principal address.

(a) Any trade union or employers' association which refuses or wilfully neglects to perform any of these duties shall be guilty of an offence for which the maximum punishment on summary conviction is £100. An offence committed under this section by a trade union or an employers' association shall also be deemed to have been committed by the officer who is bound by the rules to perform that duty. It will be a defence for such officer for him to prove that he had reasonable grounds to believe, and did believe, that some other person who was competent and reliable, was authorised to perform that duty instead of him: section 91.

(b) If any person with intent to enable a trade union or employers' association to evade any of the above provisions, or, with intent to falsify, wilfully alters any document which is required for any of those provisions, he will be guilty of an offence. The maximum penalty is a fine on summary conviction not exceeding £400: section 91.   **[335]**

(iii) Section 158 (3) provides that if proceedings are being heard before the NIRC or an industrial tribunal in private, no information given by any person in evidence shall be disclosed to anyone except with the consent of the person who gave that information in evidence. Any person who discloses such information contrary to that section is liable on summary conviction to a fine of £400.   **[336]**

(iv) For the purpose of conducting a ballot under the Act the CIR may require any employer to furnish them with the names and addresses of his employees, and particulars as to the positions they hold. Any person who wilfully neglects to comply, or who knowingly or recklessly makes any false material statement in respect thereof, is liable on summary conviction to a fine of up to £400: 3rd Schedule, paragraph 38 (2).   **[337]**

(v) The Registrar, and the CIR have wide powers to conduct investigations and enquiries. Any person who wilfully neglects to attend after being summoned, or who alters, suppresses, conceals, destroys or refuses to produce any book or document which he has been required to produce, or refuses or neglects to furnish any estimate, return or other information so required or makes a false material statement, shall be liable on summary conviction to a fine of £100: 3rd Schedule, paragraph 42 (4).   **[338]**

(vi) No information given or supplied by any person in connection with an enquiry made by the CIR, or by the Registrar under section 82 or section 83, shall be disclosed without that person's consent, except for certain official purposes. A person found guilty of this offence can be fined on summary conviction up to £400: 3rd Schedule, paragraph 45.   **[339]**

(vii) Regulations may be made by the Secretary of State for the purpose of proceedings before the industrial tribunals, requiring persons to attend to give evidence, to produce documents and for ordering the discovery and inspection of documents. Any person who without reasonable excuse fails to comply with any requirement imposed by the regulations may be liable on summary conviction to a fine not exceeding £100: 6th Schedule, paragraph 11.   **[340]**

E. RESIDUAL LIABILITY—PICKETING (section 134)

If one or more persons, in contemplation or furtherance of an industrial dispute, attend at or near:

(a) a place where a person works or carries on business; or
(b) any other place where a person happens to be, not being a place where he resides,

and do so only for the purpose of peacefully obtaining information from him, or peacefully communicating information to him, or peacefully persuading him to work or not to work, then, such action shall not of itself constitute:

> (i) an offence under section 7 of the Conspiracy and Protection of Property Act 1875 (penalty for intimidation or annoyance by violence), or under any other enactment or rule of law, and,
> (ii) a tort: section 134.   [341]

In other words, the protection given to peaceful picketing by the 1906 Act is continued, with the exception that this must not take place at the home of the person who is being picketed. If nothing else is done other than the statutory objects, peaceful picketing is lawful. However, this does not permit pickets to obstruct the highway,[16] and a police constable who anticipates a breach of the peace may restrict the number of pickets who may be placed at the premises.[17] If violence is used, or if there is intimidation, then criminal and civil liabilities may arise.   [342]

Other criminal penalties

It is, perhaps, worth noting that the Industrial Relations Act repeals section 4 of the Conspiracy and Protection of Property Act 1875, and section 31 of the Electricity (Supply) Act 1919. These sections made it a criminal offence for persons in the gas, water or electricity industries to break their contracts of employment (e.g., by going on strike, or going-slow, but not a work to rule) knowing that the probable consequence was to deprive persons of the supply of these amenities.   [343]

However, section 5 of the Conspiracy and Protection of Property Act 1875 still exists. This makes it a criminal offence for a person to *break* his contract of employment, the probable consequence of which is to endanger human life, or cause serious bodily injury, or to expose valuable property to destruction or injury. (But see Chapter 8.)   [344]

The Police Act 1964 provides that it shall be a criminal offence to do anything likely to cause dissatisfaction, breach of discipline, or the withdrawal of labour of the police force: section 53.   [345]

---

[16] *Tynan* v. *Balmer*, [1967] 1 Q.B. 91.
[17] *Piddington* v. *Bates*, [1960] 3 All E.R. 660.

CHAPTER SIX

EMERGENCY PROCEDURES

Two provisions giving the Government additional powers to deal with national emergencies caused by industrial disputes were enacted in the Industrial Relations Act. **[346]**

A. "COOLING OFF" PERIOD (sections 138–140)

If it appears to the Secretary of State that:

(i) in contemplation of furtherance of an industrial dispute, industrial action (i.e., a strike or irregular industrial action or a lock-out) has begun or is likely to begin;

(ii) that the industrial action has or would cause an interruption in the supply of goods or the provision of services of such nature, or on such a scale, as to be likely

(a) to be gravely injurious to the national economy, to imperil national security or to create a serious risk of public disorder; or

(b) to endanger the lives of a substantial number of persons, or to expose a substantial number of persons to serious risk of disease or personal injury; and

(iii) that having regard to all the circumstances of the industrial dispute, it would be conducive to a settlement of it by negotiation, conciliation or arbitration if the industrial action was discontinued or deferred,

then the Secretary of State may apply to the Industrial Court for an order. The application shall specify the persons responsible for the strike or lock-out, and those persons shall be parties to any proceedings on the application. **[347]**

If the NIRC is satisfied on the evidence that there are sufficient grounds for believing that either condition set out in (ii) (a) or (b) above is fulfilled, it shall make an order specifying:

(a) the area of employment;
(b) the persons who are bound by the order; and
(c) the date on which it is to take effect and the period, not exceeding sixty days, for which it is to remain in force.

The NIRC will not make an order against persons who have no responsibility for any strike or irregular industrial action in question other than the fact that they are taking part in it, or have no responsibility for calling, organising, procuring or financing the strike or other irregular industrial action, except in their capacity as officials of a trade union acting within the scope of their authority. In other words, a NIRC order will not be made against actual strikers, nor against a trade union official who, acting in the course of his duties, calls or threatens to call for industrial action. This means that officials of unregistered organisations of workers, unofficial strike leaders, etc., can be made the subjects of NIRC orders, as well as trade unions themselves. The NIRC order will direct that during the period it is in force, no person specified therein shall:

(a) call, organise, procure or finance a strike, or threaten to do so; or
(b) organise, procure or finance any irregular industrial action, or threaten to do so; or
(c) institute, carry on, authorise or finance a lock-out, or threaten to do so,

within the area of employment so specified.   **[348]**

The order may also require the withdrawal of any such instruction or other steps to secure that the industrial action is discontinued or deferred during the period to which the order relates.   **[349]**

The order may be for a period less than sixty days, but, on an application by the Secretary of State, it may be extended, not, however, so as to exceed sixty days in all. The Secretary of State may also apply for inclusion of other persons in the order in certain special circumstances; such supplementary order may direct the withdrawal of any instructions of industrial action, or other steps to be taken to secure the discontinuance or deferrment of such action. Other than these special cases, once the NIRC has made its principal order, it cannot entertain any other application relating to the same industrial dispute.   **[350]**

B. STRIKE BALLOTS (sections 141–145)

If it appears to the Secretary of State:

(i) that in contemplation of furtherance of a trade dispute a strike or other irregular industrial action has begun or is likely to begin:

(ii) that the industrial action has or would cause an interruption in the supply of goods or the provision of services of such a nature or on such a scale, as to be likely

(a) to be gravely injurious to the national economy, to imperil national security or to create a serious risk of public disorder; or

(b) to endanger the lives of a substantial number of persons or to expose a substantial number of persons to serious risk of disease or personal injury; *and/or*

(iii) the effects of the industrial action on a particular industry are, or are likely to be, such as to be seriously injurious to the livelihood of a substantial number of workers employed in that industry; *and*

(iii) there are reasons for doubting whether the workers who are taking part or who are expected to take part in the industrial action are (or would be) taking part in accordance with their wishes, and there is a doubt whether they have had an adequate opportunity of indicating their wishes in this respect,

then, the Secretary of State may apply to the NIRC for an order requiring that a ballot be held. Before making the application, he must, so far as is practicable, consult every employer, trade union or employers' association appearing to him to be a party to the industrial dispute in question (it will be noted, therefore, that he need not consult any unregistered organisation of workers or employers, though there is nothing to stop him doing so should he wish). If the NIRC is satisfied that either or both of the conditions (ii) and (iii) above are fulfilled, it will order a ballot. The order will specify the persons to be balloted (whether by reference to the industry, the undertaking or the description of the workers), the question on which the ballot is to be taken and the period within which the result is to be reported to the NIRC. The assistance of the CIR may be invoked for the purpose of formulating any such order. **[351]**

During the period beginning with the date on which the order takes effect, and ending with the date on which the result of the ballot is reported to the NIRC:

(a) no organisation of workers, or officials or any other person

118

specified in the order shall do or threaten to do anything which involves anything by way of strike or irregular industrial action, and
(b) no employer or organisation of employers or person specified in the order shall invoke a lock-out of these workers.   [352]

The order may also require any organisation or official or other person so specified to withdraw any instructions relating to the industrial action, and any other steps for the purpose of ensuring its discontinuance or deferment during the period stated above.

During this time, the Secretary of State may apply for the inclusion within the order of other persons who may be responsible for taking some form of industrial action, and the NIRC order will extend to them as if they had been parties to the original application. Again, actual strikers and officials of trade unions who are involved in the dispute cannot be made the subject of a NIRC order.   [354]

The responsibility for holding the ballot is with the CIR. If some or all of the persons eligible to vote are members of a trade union which is recognised by the employer as having negotiating rights in respect of those workers, and the union is one whose rules have been approved by the Registrar, the CIR may request the trade union to hold the ballot, and if it does so, the ballot will be conducted in accordance with those rules, and the result reported to the CIR. The CIR shall pay any expenses reasonably incurred. Otherwise, the CIR will conduct or supervise the ballot, and in any case, shall be responsible for ensuring that the questions on the ballot is in accordance with the NIRC order. Any doubt as to how the order is to be interpreted or applied shall be determined by the CIR, subject to an application being made to the NIRC by any person who was a party to the proceedings before the NIRC. Finally, the CIR will report the result of the ballot to the NIRC, and the court will publish this in an appropriate manner. It will be noted that from thence on, the NIRC order lapses, and anyone is free to take any form of industrial action, subject to the general provisions of the Act, and the ordinary law of the land.   [355]

Other powers

The Industrial Relations Act in no way affects the powers of the Government to act under the previous law. These include conciliation and arbitration powers (with the consent of both sides), and the setting up of courts of enquiry and committees of investigation (Conciliation Act 1896 and Industrial Court Act 1919). Equally, the Emergency Powers Act 1920 still exists on the statute book.   [356]

CHAPTER SEVEN

INDIVIDUAL RIGHTS

So far we have been considering the Industrial Relations Act in respect of its impact on group rights and group conflicts. In many ways, however, perhaps the most significant effect of the Act may well be in the way it provides for the individual worker in industry. [357]

A. RIGHTS IN RESPECT OF TRADE UNIONISM (section 5 (1))

Section 5 (1) provides that as between himself and his employer, every worker shall have the right to belong to any trade union of his choice, the right to take part in the activities of that trade union at the appropriate time (including activities which may lead to him becoming an official (e.g., a shop steward), the right to seek and accept appointment or election to office, and to hold such office.[1] [358]

The term "worker" means a person who works or seeks to work:

(a) under a contract of employment;

(b) under any other contract whereby he undertakes to perform personally any work or services (except of a professional nature);

(c) in Crown employment (other than the armed forces). [359]

The term is thus wider than "employee", and consequently covers a larger area of employment. Independent contractors, labour-only sub-contractors, apprentices, come within the scope of section 5 (1). Supposing an employer engages a group of "labour only" sub-contractors, and stipulates that they shall not be members of a trade union. This will be an unfair industrial practice on his part, even though those workers are not his own employees. [360]

The term "at the appropriate time" means time which is outside his working hours, or time which is set aside in accordance with

---

[1] Apparantly this does not include activities on a public body which may arise out of trade union activities, e.g. service as a local councillor, or school governor, though it is possible that this may be included in the Code of Practice at some future date.

arrangements made with, or consented to, by or on behalf of the employer, for such activities to be conducted. It is unlikely that many employers will seek to restrict the right of a worker to take part in trade union activities outside his working hours, but some employers will not accept that the recruiting of members, or the collection of subscriptions, or the holding of meetings, may be done in working hours. In order, therefore, that the protection of section 5 (1) shall apply, it will be necessary for some agreement to be entered into by the trade union (or the worker) and the employer stating what time may be set aside for such activities, or in the absence of a specific time, then a statement of the trade union activities which may be conducted by the worker in working hours generally.   [361]

It will be noted that the section only guarantees the right in respect of trade unions (including those on the provisional register): a worker who wishes to exercise his freedom to join an organisation of workers which is not registered as a trade union is not protected by the section.   [362]

Although the term "worker" is fairly comprehensive, it does not cover a group of persons who are technically known as "office holders". The most important section of this group are the police, special constables and other members of the constabulary (e.g. railway police, etc.) who, because they are not workers within the statutory definition, cannot claim the rights contained in section 5 (1). The Police Act 1964, section 4 (1) generally forbids police officers to join trade unions or other associations having for its objects, or one of its objects, to control or influence the pay, pensions or conditions of service of any police force, and it will be recalled that the Industrial Relations Act does not give the right to join an organisation of workers (whether it is, or is not, an association within the meaning of the Police Act). Members of the police force, however, may join the Police Federation, though this organisation is not eligible for registration under any of the provisions of the Industrial Relations Act because it does not have the power to alter its own rules (this may only be done by the Secretary of State, see the Police Act 1964, section 44 (3)). However, section 164 (3) of the Industrial Relations Act empowers the Secretary of State to provide that the word "worker" shall include certain specified office holders, in which case the provisions of section 5 (1) will apply to them. Should this ever be done with reference to the police, there will be an implied repeal of section 47 (1) of the Police Act. The constitution of the Police Federation, however, will have to be revised should it wish to register as a trade union under the Industrial Relations Act.   [363]

Every worker also has the right not to join a trade union or other organisation of workers, either generally or in respect of a particular trade union or organisation. (This provision has been stated to the implementation of the Universal Declaration of Human Rights, which provides that no person shall be compelled to join an organisation). However, this right not to join is qualified in those circumstances where an agency shop agreement is in existence. A worker may refuse to join the union only if he agrees to pay the appropriate contribution to the trade union in lieu of membership, or, if he is a conscientious objector, pays an equivalent of the union subscription to an agreed charity. Similarly, if there is an approved closed shop agreement in force, he must either join the union or pay his appropriate contribution to a charity.   **[364]**

Section 5 (1) is not without its problems. Supposing an employer says to a worker "I would like to promote you to foreman, but you are an active member of a trade union, and there may be a conflict between your union activities and my own interests". Has the worker been penalised or discriminated against? It is not an unfair industrial practice for the employer to encourage workers to join a trade union with which he negotiates, but is it an unfair industrial practice to gently discourage (as opposed to deter)? It will be an unfair industrial practice to pay trade union members less than non-members, if the reason was because they exercised their rights to be members, but there are many reasons why an employer may pay a particular worker more than another, and it may not be easy to prove such discrimination. If an employer offers to his workers a benefit by way of an inducement to refrain from exercising any of the rights in section 5 (1), and he gives that benefit to those who agree to refrain from exercising those rights, and withholds it from those who do not agree, this will amount to an act of discrimination, which will be an unfair industrial practice: section 5 (4). Thus, if an employer offers to pay workmen higher wages if they leave a trade union, and he actually carries out that promise, then he is discriminating against those who have not agreed to leave the union (but not, of course, if the union was unregistered). Curiously enough, the reverse situation is equally applicable. Some employers have been known to offer inducements in order to get workmen to join a particular trade union, by offering higher wages to union workers only. In respect of non-unionists, therefore, this will now amount to an act of discrimination. However, such inducement only becomes discrimination if it relates to the exercise of a right conferred by section 5 (1). An employer who offers to pay workers more money if they abstain from going on strike, or if they return to work, does not commit an act of discrimination within the meaning of section 5 (4).   **[365]**

Unfair industrial practice (**section 5 (2))**

It will be unfair industrial practice for any employer, or any person acting on his behalf, to prevent or deter a worker exercising any of the rights protected by section 5 (1), or to dismiss, penalise or otherwise discriminate against him by reason of his exercising such a right, or to refuse to engage him on the grounds that he is a member of a trade union, or not a member of a trade union or other organisation of workers. If, however, an agency shop agreement is in force, it will be perfectly lawful for an employer (or person acting on his behalf) to dismiss, penalise or discriminate against such a worker on the grounds that he is not a member of that trade union, and has not agreed, or has refused (or failed) to pay his appropriate contribution to the union or an agreed charity. The employer may also refuse to engage a worker who would be the subject of an agency shop agreement on the grounds that he is not a member of that trade union and refuses to join or to pay the appropriate contribution to the trade union or the charity: section 6.   **[366]**

Equally, if there is an approved closed shop agreement in force, it will be perfectly lawful for the employer to dismiss, penalise or otherwise discriminate against a worker covered by the agreement on the grounds that he is not a member of the appropriate trade union, and has refused to join it, or has been excluded from it, or refuses to pay the appropriate contribution to a charity: section 17. A failure on the part of the employer to pay a contribution to a trade union or charity under the check-off system will not be regarded as a failure to pay the contribution by the worker. The employer may also refuse to engage a non-unionist who refuses to join, or has been excluded from the union. The worker, of course, must apply for membership of the union within the appropriate period (three months in respect of workers employed at the time the agreement was made, and one month from the commencement of employment in respect of new workers). He will be treated as having been excluded from the union if:

(a) his application for membership has been rejected, or, if he was a member, he has been expelled; and
(b) his appeal against the rejection or expulsion has been dismissed or withdrawn, or the time for appealing expired without his making an appeal.

Thus a worker who does not try to join the union may be dismissed, whereas one who has applied to join is entitled not to be dismissed until his application or expulsion is disposed of in accordance with the circumstances.   **[367]**

It would appear that it is not an unfair industrial practice to refuse to engage a conscientious objector in an approved closed shop situation, even though he is willing to pay an appropriate contribution to a charity. This anomalous result stems from the wording of section 17 (5) (b). Conscientious objectors, therefore, can only rely on their statutory rights in a situation where there is an agency shop agreement in force, or no agreement at all.   **[368]**

It will be recalled (see para. **[209]**, *ante*) that informal, or bogus closed shop agreements are void, and a worker who is prevented from obtaining employment because of the existence of such an agreement may apply to the NIRC for a declaration that the agreement is void: section 7. He must show that the agreement, however expressed, is designed to defeat the object of the Act, that the refusal of the employer to engage him was wholly or partly attributable to that agreement, and that the effect is to constitute a substantial derogation from his rights not to be a member of an organisation of workers. Thus, supposing an agreement states that employment of any particular worker shall be subject to the approval of a local committee, all of whom are known to be communists, the practical effect of this agreement is to enforce a closed shop, and any worker refused employment may take the matter to the NIRC. However, section 7 does not prevent an employer imposing as a pre-condition of employment a specific qualification, or that the applicant shall have certain experience. Thus a professional closed shop may be maintained by virtue of qualifications and/or membership of the professional organisation, whether or not it is an organisation of workers (including a specially registered body). Any remedy the worker may have (if at all) can thus be pursued under section 65 (see Chapter 2).   **[369]**

It will also be unfair industrial practice for any person (including a trade union or other organisation of workers or any official thereof) by calling, organising, procuring or financing a strike, or by organising, procuring or financing any irregular industrial action short of a strike, or threatening to do either, knowingly to induce or attempt to induce an employer or someone acting on his behalf, to do anything which as stated above would be an unfair industrial practice on the part of the employer: section 33 (3). The commonest form this would take would be a strike or go-slow, designed to compel a worker to join the union in a non-agency shop situation under threat of dismissal but there are a number of other possibilities, particularly in respect of the activities of organisations of workers.   **[370]**

B. PROTECTION AGAINST UNFAIR DISMISSAL
(sections 22–30)

Section 22 provides that (subject to certain exceptional cases, for which see below) every employee shall have the right not to be unfairly dismissed by his employer,[2] and an employer who dismissed an employee unfairly is guilty of an unfair industrial practice. The term "employee" means an individual who has entered into or works under a contract of employment, and the term has a more restricted meaning than the word "worker" which is used in the Act (see above). "Workers", however, may still pursue any remedy which is available under the existing law.[3]   **[371]**

A person will be regarded as having been dismissed if the contract under which he is employed is terminated by the employer (with or without notice), or, if he is under a fixed term contract, the term expires without being renewed. Thus an employer who makes working life "difficult", if not impossible, for the employee, thus bringing about a situation where the latter resigns, has not dismissed him within the meaning of the Act. If, while the employee is "working" his notice, he gives a counter notice in writing that he intends to leave on a date earlier than the date when his notice expires, he will still be regarded as having been dismissed by the employer for the reasons given by the employer.   **[372]**

It is for the employer to show what was the reason for the dismissal, and that it was a reason specified below or some other substantial reason sufficient to justify the dismissal of an employee holding the position which he held: section 24. Thus if the employer gives no reason, it will be unfair dismissal. The dismissal may be fair if it is made for any of the following reasons:

(a) that it relates to the capability or qualifications of the employee for performing work of the kind which he was employed to do. "Capability" may be assessed by reference to the skill, aptitude, health, or any physical or mental quality, and "qualifications" means any academic, technical, or professional qualifications relevant to the position which the employee holds. Thus an employee who is persistently sick, or who has been struck off a relevant professional society's list of members, may be fairly dismissed under this section;

---

[2] Teachers in voluntary aided schools who are dismissed by the governors are, for the purpose of the relevant provisions, to be regarded as having been employed by the local education authority: section 148. This is necessary in order to prevent the governors of such schools raising the defence of section 24 (2) (d).

[3] See *Dunk* v. *Waller & Sons Ltd.*, [1970] 2 All E.R. 630.

(b) that it relates to the conduct of the employee. Thus an employee who "skylarks about" may be dismissed if such conduct interferes with the work, or is a danger to other employees.[4] However, there is no requirement that the conduct in question should relate solely to matters arising out of the course of the employment. Thus if a cashier is convicted of stealing funds from the local amateur dramatics society, this may throw such doubt on his honesty as to warrant a fair dismissal within the section. The husband of Lady Chatterly would not have been guilty of unfair dismissal if he had fired the gamekeeper!;

(c) that the employee was redundant. Here, we must consider the effects of the Redundancy Payments Act 1965;

(d) that the employee could not continue to work in the position without contravening (either on his part or on the part of the employer) a duty or restriction imposed by or under an enactment. Thus a person who is employed to drive a van may be dismissed because he has lost his driving licence.

Whatever the reason for the dismissal, whether one of the above reasons or other substantial reason, the determination of the question whether the dismissal was fair or unfair, having regard to the reason given by the employer, shall depend on whether in the circumstances he acted reasonably or unreasonably in treating it as a sufficient reason for dismissing the employee, and that question will be determined in accordance with equity and the substantial merits of the case. Thus even when a good reason for dismissal is shown (including any of the four reasons (a)–(d) mentioned above) the dismissal shall still be regarded as being unfair if in the circumstances the employer acted unreasonably in treating it as a sufficient reason for dismissal. This provision is likely to cause a lot of difficulty, for it amounts to saying that although the employer had a good reason for dismissing an employee, he acted unreasonably in treating it as a good reason. It is possible, however, to tentatively suggest that some of the old law on summary dismissal may well be relevant here. Thus, supposing an employee is dismissed because he swore in vulgar terms at the foreman. The reason would relate to the conduct (see above (b)) but the courts have held that the test to be applied is the standards of men, not of angels![5] Equally, if the dismissal is made because the employee was occasionally late for work, or persistently late, then whether this amounts to a sufficient reason for dismissal will be a question of fact, having regard to the nature of the

---

[4] *Hudson* v. *Ridge Manufacturing Co.*, [1951] 2 Q.B. 348.
[5] *Jupiter General Insurance Co.* v. *Shroff*, [1937] 3 All E.R. 37.

employment, the provisions of any agreement between the employer and the unions or employees, previous warnings, treatment of like cases by the employer, and so forth. The tribunals, which will have to deal with unfair dismissal cases, are likely to take the view that remarks made in the heat of the moment are not sufficient to warrant dismissal, provided the relationship between the parties is capable of being restored. Further, all questions on unfair dismissal shall be determined in accordance with equity and the substantial merits of the case, which may involve the tribunals in a deep examination of complex issues involving human relations in an industrial atmosphere.   [373]

On the other hand, a dismissal will be unfair if the reason or principle reason was:

(i) that the employee has exercised his rights, or indicated his intention to exercise his rights, under section 5 (1) (right to join or not to join a trade union, see above);

(ii) if he was dismissed for redundancy, and the circumstances were such that the redundancy could have applied to other employees, but they were not dismissed, and the reason he was selected for dismissal was that he exercised, or indicated his intention to exercise his rights under section 5 (1), or he was selected for dismissal in contravention of a customary arrangement for agreed procedure relating to redundancy, and there were no special reasons justifying a departure from that procedure in his case. Thus an employer cannot use the excuse of redundancy to obtain the dismissal of a trade union activist. He can, however, dismiss an employee who is an active member of an unregistered organisation of workers, for section 5 (1) does not confer any right to be a member of such an organisation.   [374]

(a) *Dismissal as a result of a strike or a lock-out* (section 26)

We must first examine the effect of strike action on the contract of employment, and then we will relate it to subsequent developments which may take place by way of a strike or lock-out.   [375]

A strike, whether official or unofficial, whether in breach of procedure or in accordance with procedure, is almost always a breach of the individual's contract of employment, in that it amounts to a breach of the employee's duty at common law to serve his employer faithfully. This is the strict legal position, and the remedy available to the employer in respect of an employee who is in breach of his contract is to treat the contract as being at an end. Thus an employer who sacks strikers is acting within his legal rights. Because strike action simpliciter is a breach of contract, (which gave rise in some cases to consequential legal liabilities, see, e.g., *Rookes* v. *Barnard*[6]) many trade unions have adopted the practice of giving "notice" of strike action, the notice usually being equal to, or exceeding the length of the time required by the employees to terminate their contract of employment. Thus by doing so, it was thought that they were not "breaking" their contract of employment. But it is equally clear that termination was not what they wanted either! This confusion was cleared up in *Morgan* v. *Fry*,[7] where Lord Denning held that due notice of strike action does not amount to the repudiation by the workers of the contract of employment, and this view is confirmed by the Act: section 147: see Chapter 8.   **[376]**

Thus, the normal remedies available to an employer whose employees are on strike are two-fold; in the first place, he may sue for damages for breach of contract (this is always an unlikely event, but see Chapter 8); secondly, he may treat the contract as being at an end. In other words, the breach of contract by the employees entitled the employer to terminate the contract. It is in this connection that the Industrial Relations Act lays down certain rules as to what constitutes "fair" and "unfair" dismissal.   **[381]**

Section 26 provides that if the reason (or principal reason) for the dismissal was that the claimant took part in strike or irregular industrial action, this dismissal shall not be regarded as being unfair, unless it can be shown that:

(a) other employees of that employer also took part in the relevant industrial action, and they were not dismissed; or

(b) other employees who were dismissed were offered re-engagement, but the claimant was not.

In this case, however, the claimant must show additionally that the principal reason why he was not offered re-engagement was that he had exercised, or indicated his intention to exercise any of the rights conferred by section 5 (1) (right to join and partake in trade union activities or right not to join the union, etc. (see above)). Thus the Act attempts to avoid victimisation of trade union workers by providing that such dismissals by the employer would be unfair.
          [382]

(b) *Dismissal in connection with a lock-out* (**section 25**)

Although legal authority is slender on the point (see *Cummings* v. *Connell & Co. Ltd.,* 1969 S.L.T. 25) there can be little doubt that a lock-out is equally a breach of contract by an employer. Again, however, the point is of academic interest, though relevant

[6] [1964] A.C. 1129.
[7] [1968] 2 Q.B. 710.

in assessing consequent actions. Section 25 provides that a dismissal by way of lock-out, whether the dismissal takes place at the beginning or during the course of a lock-out shall not be regarded as being unfair, if the employee is offered re-engagement from the date of the resumption of work. Re-engagement may be offered in the position the employee held before the lock-out, or a different position which is reasonably suitable, and may be made by the same employer, or his successor or an associated employer. If an employee is not offered re-engagement, the provisions of section 24 (above) apply as if the reason for dismissal there were substituted the reasons for not offering re-engagement.   **[383]**

(c) *Excluded cases* **(section 27)**

The protection against unfair dismissal does not apply to a number of specified cases. These are as follows:

(a) Undertakings which employ less than four employees who were employed for more than thirteen weeks (including the claimant). Supposing two employees work on a farm. In the summer, there may be an increase in casual labour to help with gathering in the crops. The requirement that there must be four employees working for at least thirteen weeks is designed to prevent the permanent employees from acquiring rights during the short season only, and leaving them without these rights for the rest of the year. Having decided that small employment groups are to be excluded, the legislature has at least been consistant.

(b) Any employment where the employer is the husband or wife or close relative of the claimant.

(c) Registered dock workers.

(d) Share fisherman.

(e) Certain teachers employed in Scotland.

(f) Employees who work less than 21 hours per week.

(g) Employees who normally work outside Great Britain.   **[384]**

Further, in order to qualify for the rights under section 22, the claimant must have been employed continuously by the employer for two years, and must be below the normal retiring age for the position which he held, or below the age of 65 (if a man) or 60 (if a woman). These exceptions and exception (a) above, do not apply if the reason for the dismissal is in connection with the rights guaranteed by section 5 (1) (relating to trade union activity), and a dismissal in these circumstances will be regarded as being unfair.   **[385]**

As noted above, the refusal to renew a contract made for a fixed term may amount to unfair dismissal, but the Act provides two exceptions to this. The first relates to a contract for two years or more which is made before the Act comes into force (not being a contract of apprenticeship) and the contract is not renewed. Secondly if the contract is for two years or more, (whether it is made before or after the Act) and the *employee*, before the term expires, agrees in writing to forgo any claim in respect of his rights under section 22. In either of these situations, if the dismissal consists solely in the failure of the employer to renew the contract it will not be unfair.

[386]

(d) *Unfair industrial practices* (section 33)

It will be an unfair industrial practice for any person to call, organise, procure or finance, strike action or to organise, procure or finance irregular industrial action if the purpose is knowingly to induce an employer to take action which would be an unfair industrial practice on his part by virtue of section 5 or section 22, on the part of the employer. Thus, if a dismissal would be unfair if made by an employer, it becomes an unfair industrial action (by strike or other such action) knowingly to induce an employer to make such a dismissal. Therefore a strike called to force the dismissal of a worker because he is not a member of a particular organisation of workers (except in an agency shop or approved closed shop situation) will be an unfair industrial action.   [387]

(e) *Exclusion in respect of a procedure agreement* (section 31)

Some units of employment already have their own procedure for dealing with dismissal cases (e.g. universities). In these cases, an application may be made to the NIRC by all the parties to the procedure agreement requesting the court to make an exempting order. The request will be granted if the court is satisfied that:

(a) every organisation of workers which is a party to the agreement is an independent organisation;

(b) the procedure agreement provides for the procedure to be followed in cases where an employee claims that he has been, or is in the course of being, unfairly dismissed;

(c) those procedures are available without discrimination to all employees falling within any description to which the procedure agreement applies;

(d) the remedies provided by the procedure agreement in respect of unfair dismissal are on the whole as beneficial as those provided by the Act, though they need not necessarily be the same;

(e) the procedure agreement includes a right to arbitration by an independent referee or tribunal or other body in cases

130

where a decision cannot be reached because there is a failure
to agree;
(f) the provisions of the procedure agreement are such that it
can be determined with reasonable certainty whether a
particular employee is covered by it.   [388]

Once the exempting order has been made, the provisions of the
procedure agreement relating to unfair dismissal shall apply in
substitution for any of the rights under section 22. However, any
party to the procedure agreement or the Secretary of State may
apply for the exemption order to be revoked. If the NIRC is satisfied
that it is the desire of all the parties that the order should be revoked,
or it comes to the conclusion that the agreement fails to fulfil all
the above conditions, then the NIRC will revoke the exempting
order. The NIRC may make transitional arrangements as it thinks fit.
[389]

(f) *Remedies for breach of section 5 or section 22* (**section 106**)
A complaint may be presented to the Industrial Tribunal against
any employer by a complainant alleging:

(i) that certain action was taken by the employer or someone
acting on his behalf;
(ii) that in accordance with section 5 (1) or section 22 that action
constituted an unfair industrial practice; and
(iii) if the complaint relates to dismissal, that he was dismissed;
otherwise, the complaint will specify that he was prevented or
deterred from exercising his rights or was penalised, or discriminated
against, or refused employment as the case may be.   [390]

If the complaint does not relate to dismissal, and the Industrial
Tribunal finds it justified, the tribunal, if it thinks just and equitable,
may award either or both of the following remedies:

(a) an order determining the rights of the complainant and of the
employer in relation to the action specified in the complaint;
(b) an award of compensation to be paid by the employer to the
complainant in respect of the action.   [391]

If the complaint relates to unfair dismissal under section 22, and
the tribunal finds that the grounds are well founded and it considers
that it would be practical, in accordance with equity, for the complainant to be re-engaged by the employer (or by his successor or an
associated employer), the tribunal shall make a recommendation
to the effect, stating the terms on which it considers it would be

131

reasonable for the complainant to be so employed. It will be noted that the tribunal can only recommend re-engagement; it cannot recommend re-instatement, though the fact that it can specify the terms on which re-engagement is to be recommended may militate against any hardship which may otherwise occur. There is no reason why a tribunal should not recommend the payment of back-pay in appropriate circumstances. It was thought that re-instatement may not always be a possible remedy, e.g., if there has been a change in the employer's circumstances, or a re-organisation of the work. Further, re-instatement may make it more difficult to get the parties to agree, particularly if personal feelings are involved. If the tribunal does not make a recommendation of re-engagement, or if it is made, but (for whatever reason) not complied with by the employer, then an award of compensation shall be made. However, it will not be an unfair industrial practice for an organisation of workers to take strike or other action to compel the re-engagement (but not re-instatement) of an employee whom the tribunal has held was unfairly dismissed, but whom the employer has refused to re-engage.   [392]

If a worker is for whatever reason dismissed penalised or otherwise discriminated against as a result of pressure which was put on the employer by means of a strike or irregular industrial action (or the threat thereof), then no account shall be taken of that pressure in determining the question (section 33 (1)), which will be decided as if the pressure was not exercised. Thus, if an employer was to claim that he was "forced" to dismiss a worker because of the threat of a strike, the matter will be determined by the tribunal as if no such threat existed, and if, as a result, the dismissal was unfair, the above remedies will follow. If the pressure amounted to an unfair industrial practice, the employer may join those responsible as parties in the proceedings, and if the tribunal finds that the pressure existed, and it was an unfair industrial practice, it may make an order requiring those responsible to make a contribution to the employer in respect of such an amount as it thinks just and equitable, even to the extent of constituting a complete indemnity section 119.: However, no such contribution order can be made against a trade union official acting in the scope of his authority, though this does not affect the power of the tribunal to make such an award against the trade union itself.   [393]

A complaint to the Industrial Tribunal under section 106 is essentially one being brought against the employer. Thus, if a trade union calls a strike against the employment of a non-unionist, and in consequence, the employer dismissed him, this may be an unfair industrial practice under section 5 (2) (b). Whether the employer dismisses him or not, an action will lie by the complainant against the trade union in respect of the unfair industrial practice committed contrary to section 33 (3) (a). This complaint may be brought to the NIRC under section 101, not to the Industrial Tribunal under 106. The advantage in doing so is that the NIRC can make an order directing the trade union to refrain from taking further such action in respect of the complainant. It is unlikely that the NIRC would award damages in addition to those obtained (if any) in the Industrial Tribunal.   [394]

(g) *Compensation* (sections 116 and 118)

The amount of compensation which may be awarded will be the amount the tribunal thinks just and equitable, having regard to the loss sustained in consequence of the matters complained of, in so far as that loss was attributed to the employer or person acting for him. This will include any expenses reasonably incurred by him, and the loss of any benefit which he might reasonably be expected to have had. Thus, if an employee who has 20 years service behind him is dismissed unfairly, it is proper to consider the fact that he has lost 20 years potential redundancy pay. Equally, the loss of pension rights may be taken into account.   [395]

Further, in all questions of compensation, the NIRC and the industrial tribunals are directed to consider the extent to which (if at all) the complainant's conduct caused or contributed to the matter complained of, and may reduce its assessment of the loss as is considered to be just and equitable. If a complainant refuses an offer of re-engagement, and this refusal is thought to be unreasonable the tribunal again can reduce the assessment of the loss; on the other hand, if the employer refuses to re-engage the complainant after the tribunal has so recommended, this may be grounds for increasing the assessment.   [396]

However, the Act provides that the employee is under the normal common law duty to mitigate against his loss. This means that a dismissed person must not take the dismissal as an opportunity for an extended holiday, but must look around for reasonably suitable alternative employment. For example, in *Brace* v. *Calder*,[8] the plaintiff was employed as a manger by a partnership. The partnership was dissolved, and he was offered re-engagement by the new owners. He refused, and sued for wrongful dismissal. It was held that he was entitled only to nominal damages, for he had unreasonably rejected the offer of re-employment in his old job at the old terms.   [397]

---

[8] [1895] 2 Q.B. 253.

133

Section 118 provides that the maximum compensation which shall be payable in respect of an application under sections 5 and 22, is the amount which represents 104 weeks pay, or £4,160, which ever is the less. The Secretary of State has the power to make orders by statutory instrument to increase this amount. **[398]**

It should be remembered that the above provisions deal with unfair dismissal. Nothing in the Act in any way affects the old law of *wrongful* dismissal. Thus if the cashier who stole the funds of the local dramatics society is sacked, he must still be given the notice to which he is entitled by the terms of his contract or under the Contracts of Employment Act (as amended), and an action to obtain such sums as are due may still be brought in the ordinary courts. Similarly, a highly paid employee who feels that he is entitled to a sum in excess of £4,160 still retains the right to sue under the old law. An employee who is "locked-out" may also sue for breach of contract, and, if he decides to regard the lock-out as a repudiation, may sue for damages. **[399]**

(h) For the rights of an individual against an organisation of workers, see Chapter 2, above.

C. OTHER MATTERS CONCERNING THE CONTRACT OF EMPLOYMENT: CONTRACTS OF EMPLOYMENT ACT 1963

The Act makes a number of minor amendments to the Contracts of Employment Act 1963 in favour of employees. The qualifying period for minimum terms of notice is reduced, and additional periods are added. The net effect is as follows: **[400]**

Employees are now entitled to the following periods of notice: if they have been employed for more than thirteen weeks, but less than two years, they must receive at least one week's notice; more than two years but less than five years' employment entitles them to two weeks' notice; more than five years but less than ten years, four weeks' notice; more than ten years but less than fifteen years, six weeks' notice, and more than fifteen years employment entitles an employee to eight weeks' notice. (Notice to terminate employment is always in addition to any other benefit to which an employee may be entitled, e.g., redundancy payments.) **[401]**

The Contracts of Employment Act also requires employers to give a written statement containing particulars of the terms of employment. In addition to the matters specified in that Act which must be given, the Industrial Relations Act requires that information shall be given not only as to holidays entitlement and holiday pay, but also the calculation of accrued holiday pay payable on the termination of the employment. The statement shall in future include a note informing the employee of his section 5 rights (to belong or not to belong to a trade union) including his rights where an agency shop or an approved closed shop is in force.   [402]

The statement must also specify the person (whether by description or otherwise) to whom the employee can apply for the purpose of seeking redress of any grievance relating to his employment, and the manner in which any such application should be made, and either explain to him the consequent steps on such application or refer him to a document which is reasonably accessible and which explains those steps.   [403]

Schedule 2 of the Industrial Relations Act makes further minor amendments to the Contracts of Employment Act.   [404]

(a) *Annual report to employees* **(section 57)**

In every undertaking in which more than 350 persons at any time during a financial year are employed (whether at the same place or a different place) the employer shall issue to his employees an annual report (not later than six months from the end of the financial year to which it relates). The report shall be sent to all employees who are employed in the undertaking on the date of its issue, except to those who work less than twenty-one hours per week, those who have been employed for less than thirteen weeks, and the employees who normally work outside Great Britain and who on the date of issue are out of the country. The Secretary of State will issue regulations specifying the information which must be given, including infomation relating to subsidiary companies and associated companies. The regulations may also exempt certain employers from this duty, and the section may be extended to include smaller firms, or limited in respect of larger firms, as the Secretary of State thinks fit.   [405]

Any person employed in the undertaking may present a complaint to the Industrial Tribunal claiming that it was the duty of the employer to issue him with such a statement, and he has failed to do so. The Tribunal may make an order determining the rights of the complainant and the employer in respect of the complaint, and may direct that the employer shall fulfill his duty within a certain period. If, at the end of that period, the employer has still not complied, the complainant may present a case to the NIRC, which may direct the employer to issue to the complainant before the end of a stated period a statement containing such information as the NIRC thinks appropriate: section 110.   [406]

(b) *Jurisdiction of Industrial Tribunals in respect of breaches of contracts of employment* **(section 113)**

It is proposed to give power to the Industrial Tribunals to hear complaints which relate to an alleged breach by either party of the contract of employment, but which is not in respect of a claim for damages for personal injuries or death. The Lord Chancellor will make orders by statutory instrument specifying the matters which may be brought before the Industrial Tribunal (subject to any specified exceptions), which would be matters which could be heard in the normal civil courts in accordance with the law for the time being in force. The Tribunal will have no power other than to award damages and costs, but it will be able to deal with the claim concurrently with any other proceedings brought before it, e.g., under the Industrial Relations Act or Redundancy Payments Act. The jurisdiction to hear cases in respect of breaches of contract of employment will be exercised concurrently with the ordinary civil courts, but an action in the latter courts may be stayed on the application of either party on the grounds that the Industrial Tribunal has the necessary jurisdiction.   [407]

The effect of this section, when it is brought into force, will mean that an employer or an employee may sue one another in the Industrial Tribunals in respect of breach of contract, but for obvious reasons this is not likely to arouse a great deal of interest on either side, except in those circumstances when the contract of employment is at an end. It should then be possible for the Industrial Tribunal to deal with all the legal issues which are outstanding between the parties, except personal injury claims.   [408]

(c) *Racial discrimination* (section 149)

By section 3 (1) of the Race Relations Act 1968, it is unlawful to refuse to employ, or to provide different terms of employment or different conditions of work, or to dismiss a person, on grounds of race, colour, ethnic or national origins. Section 149 of the Industrial Relations Act provides that the Secretary of State or the Race Relations Board shall not proceed under the Race Relations Act in respect of a complaint of an unlawful action under section 3 (1) of that Act if the matter could be dealt with by reference to the Industrial Tribunal under section 106 (above). If, on a determination of the matter by the Tribunal, it is found that the reason for the unfair industrial practice (whether an act of dismissal or otherwise) related to the complainant's colour, race, ethnic or national origins, the Secretary of State or the Race Relations Board may nonetheless seek a written assurance against a repetition of such act of discrimination, and may, if the assurance given is broken, proceed under the Race Relations Act as appropriate.   [409]

(d) *Miscellaneous matters*

Any provision in any agreement, whether a contract of employment or not, whereby the terms of the Industrial Relations Act are excluded or limited, or which purports to prevent any person from bringing a complaint before the NIRC or an Industrial Tribunal shall be void. This, however, does not apply to any agency shop or approved closed shop agreement, to fixed term contract of more than two years where the employee has agreed to waive his rights in respect of section 22 (see above), or to a procedure agreement which has been exempted by the NIRC under section 31 (above), or an agreement to refrain from proceeding with cases whilst they are dealt with by the Registrar or the conciliation officers.　　**[410]**

The Act also makes certain other minor amendments to the Redundancy Payments Act 1965 (see section 150) and the Contracts of Employment Act 1963 (see section 151). In particular, in the former case, the Secretary of State may make regulations to prevent a dismissed employee from obtaining a redundancy payment in addition to compensation for dismissal.　　**[411]**

(e) *Crown employees* **(section 162)**

The Act applies with suitable modification to Crown employees, except those who are in the armed forces. However, the full range of remedies are not available in an action against the Crown, though in practice this is not likely to cause a great deal of concern. Thus, on a complaint of an unfair industrial practice against a Minister of the Crown or government department, the only remedies available are an order of rights and an award of compensation, and even the latter is not available if the complaint refers to section 55 (1) (bargaining with an organisation of workers not recognised by a NIRC order, or failing to bargain with a trade union so recognised). If the complaint relates to a breach of duty under section 13 (1) or section 56, only an order of rights may be given. In other words, the NIRC cannot order the Crown to do or not to do a specific thing, though, in almost all cases, compensation may be awarded.

[412]

CHAPTER EIGHT

THE RIGHT TO STRIKE

Nowhere in the Industrial Relations Act are there any provisions which in any way restrict the right of an individual worker to go on strike, and indeed section 128 provided that no court shall, by way of an order for specific performance, or an injunction[1] restraining a breach of a contract of employment, compel an employee to do any work or to attend any place for the purpose of doing any work. Equally, no court shall grant an injunction to restrain an employee from working in accordance with his contract of employment in order to compel him to take part in a strike or other irregular industrial action. To ascertain the legal liability of strike action so far as individual workers are concerned, one must look at the individual contracts of employment, and the terms which are either expressed, or implied, or incorporated therein by reference to a collective agreement. At common law, a strike by an individual employee ipso facto amounts to a breach of contract of employment, in that it is a breach of the employee's duty of faithful service to his employer, and for that breach he may be dismissed summarily, or alternatively, the employer could sue for damages. The Industrial Relations Act recognises this in a number of provisions. For example, section 26 provides that such dismissal may in fact be unfair if other employees who were on strike were not dismissed, or were re-engaged. The act of going on strike does not, by itself, give rise to any unfair industrial practice, and the only criminal liability for breaking a contract of employment is contained in section 5 of the Conspiracy and Protection of Property Act 1875 (see para. [344], ante). [413]

Liability will exist, however, for those employees who induce others to go on strike in breach of their contracts, unless they are protected by section 96 (see para. [306], ante), and it is here that there is an avowed intention to impose liability on the leaders of "wild-cat" or unofficial strikes. [414]

In Scotland, specific implement or an interdict.

If an organisation of workers calls, etc., a strike which amounts to an unfair industrial practice, then liability will arise under the respective heading, which may lead to a complaint under section 101. However, if no such unfair industrial practice is committed, liability will exist for inducing a breach of contract of employment, which, by virtue of section 96, is an unfair industrial practice. We have seen, however, that trade unions and their officials are protected under that section. An organisation of workers which is not registered is not protected, and may, therefore, incur liability. Only time will tell how many organisations of workers will fail to register, but it would completely cripple their powers of industrial action if there were no circumstances in which they could call for strike action, and they would be exposed to the full rigour of the law. To meet this, a modified freedom of strike action was provided for in section 147, though whether or not the section fully meets the intentions of Parliament must remain to be seen.   **[415]**

Section 147 is so important that it must be set out and discussed in detail.

"(1) Due notice given by or on behalf of an employee of his intention to take part in a strike shall not, unless it otherwise expressly provides, be construed

(a) as a notice to terminate his contract of employment, or

(b) as a repudiation of that contract."

Due notice here means notice of a duration not less than that which the employee would be required to give to terminate his contract of employment. So, if an employee has to give four week's notice to end his contract of employment, he must give notice of strike action of at least that length if his action in striking is not to be regarded as a notice to terminate or repudiate his contract.   **[416]**

"(2) Subject to the next following subsection" (i.e., subsection 3) "where an employee takes part in a strike after due notice of his intention to do so has been given by him or on his behalf, his action in taking part in the strike shall not be regarded as a breach of his contract of employment for the purposes of—

(a) any proceedings in contract brought against the employee in respect of a breach of that contract, or

(b) any proceedings in tort, whether brought against the employee or brought against any other person, or

(c) section 5 of the Conspiracy and Protection of Property Act 1875 (breach of contract involving injury to persons or property), or

(d) section 96 of this Act."   **[417]**

Thus, once due notice of strike action has been given, subsection 2 provides four immunities from the law. In the first place, the strike will not be regarded as a breach of contract of employment *for the purpose of any proceedings brought against the employee by the employer.* The breach of contract is still there, but the employer cannot bring a successful legal action.   **[418]**

Secondly, it will be noticed that once due notice of strike action has been given, the strike will not be regarded as a breach of contract for the purpose of any action in tort. This is the immunity to which organisations of workers must look, for the action for inducing a breach of contract is an action in tort, and subsection (2) now states that the strike is not to be regarded as a breach of contract for that purpose.[2]   **[419]**

Thirdly, once due notice has been given, the strike will not amount to a breach of contract for the purposes of the Conspiracy and Protection of Property Act. Workers in all industries (be they gas, water, electricity workers, or any other) who might fall foul of that Act will escape criminal penalties if they give the requisite notice.
                              [420]

Fourthly, once due notice has been given, the strike will not amount to a breach of contract for the purpose of section 96, which, it will be recalled, makes it an unfair industrial practice to induce a breach of contract.   **[421]**

Thus, provided due notice of strike action has been given the four protections of section 147 apply, and so far as organisations of workers are concerned, there will be no liability in tort and no unfair industrial practice based on section 96. It must be borne in mind that the organisation of workers must give sufficient notice in respect of all the employees who are being called out on strike, and thus if these have different periods of notice the problem may be complicated. Suppose, in a particular undertaking, employees have to give periods of notice varying from one week to one month. The organisation of workers must either call them out in stages, in accordance with the varying periods, or give notice of strike action which is equal to the maximum period required to be given by any employee. The first method would result in only a partial stoppage and might lead to difficulties and recriminations. The second method could be equally frustrating, for if an employer managed to get one worker to agree to having to give (say) six months notice, strike action would be almost indefinitely delayed. The organisation of workers will have to make enquiries among all the employees to

---

[2] See also, section 132, which provides a defence in respect of certain acts done in contemplation or furtherance of an industrial dispute. There are, however, other tort actions possible; see Chapter 5.

ascertain what periods of notice are required to be given, for the wrongful act of inducing a breach of contract does not require knowledge of the precise terms if there is knowledge that the contract exists (see para. [309], *ante*).   [422]

However, there is one further hazard to consider.

"(3) Subsection 2 of this section shall not apply to any action by an employee which is contrary to a term of his contract of employment (including any term implied or incorporated in that contract by reference to a collective agreement) excluding or restricting his right to take part in a strike."   [423]

Supposing an employee has, in his contract of employment, an express term which states "The employee agrees that under no circumstances will he go on strike". Clearly, if he strikes in breach of that term, all the protections of subsection (2) will disappear. Suppose, further, that an organisation of workers calls him out on strike. They will be inducing a breach of contract, and will be liable under section 96.   [424]

Suppose, next, that there is a collective agreement which is expressly or impliedly incorporated into the contract of employment. If this states "The employees will not go on strike until the procedure for settling the dispute is exhausted", then a strike in breach of this term, even though due notice has been given, will again lead to the disappearance of all the protections in subsection 2. If the collective agreement goes further and states that all disputes shall be subject to a binding arbitration, then a strike by an unregistered organisation of workers becomes virtually impossible.   [425]

The real problem will arise if the relevant term of the collective agreement is contained in the procedural clauses, for we must consider the extent to which this can be incorporated into the individual contracts of employment, either expressly or impliedly. Suppose a notice given under the Contracts of Employment Act states that the terms and conditions of the employee will be determined by the agreements in force for the time being, or by reference to an agreed document (Blue Book, Brown Book, etc.). Assume further that the collective agreement states that the *union* will not call a strike until the procedure is exhausted. Can this term be incorporated into the contract of employment? The obligation may be expressed to be on the union, but, by implication, is it an obligation also on all the employees? A great deal may actually turn on the phraseology used, for in *Rookes* v. *Barnard* the terms of an agreement made between the employers' side and employees' side of a joint negotiating panel were accepted without argument as being incorporated into the contracts of employment of the individual employees. The law

141

relating to the implied incorporation of the terms of a collective agreement into the individual contract of employment is by no means fully explored, and there is yet scope for further judicial development in this field.   [426]

There is one further path which may require exploration. It will be recalled that subsection (3) removes the protection of subsection (2) if the employee is acting contrary to a term in his contract of employment excluding or restricting his right to strike. Could it be that such a term exists in every contract of employment already? After all, a strike *is* a breach of that contract,[3] and therefore the breach must be in respect of a term (implied, presumably) which places a restriction on the right to strike. It will be recalled that subsection (1) above states that if due notice is given, this is not to be construed as notice to terminate or repudiate the contract of employment. Now a person is in breach of contract if he does one of two things, namely (*a*) makes an explicit or implicit repudiation, or (*b*) fails to perform the contract at the time. Subsection (1) applies to the former case but not to the latter. The result is that although the strike notice does not amount to a repudiation, the strike, when it takes place, does amount to a breach. If this is so, then the whole protection of subsection (2) vanishes into thin air, except in respect of those employees who have some term in their contracts permitting strike action in the specified circumstances. On the other hand, it could be argued that there is an implication in modern strike law that each side is prepared to accept strike notice of a proper length, and that such notice does not give rise to any unlawful action.[4] The argument may be convincing in so far as it relates to the wrongful acts of inducing breach of contract, intimidation, etc.,[5] but it is submitted that it falls down in respect of the legal position between the employee and the employer, for so long as the latter retains the right to dismiss, he can only be dismissing a striker in respect of a breach of contract, and it does not seem to matter that notice of the intended breach was given. [427]

It is clear that the intention of Parliament was to give a limited protection to those who induce strikes provided due notice was given, though this protection was to be removed if the action nonetheless amounted to a breach of a "no strike" clause. A literal construction of section 147 suggests that the section is narrower than was intended.   [428]

---

[3] Whether the notice is given or not; see *Morgan* v. *Fry,* [1968] 2 Q.B. 710, *per* Russell, L.J.

[4] See *Morgan* v. *Fry, per* Lord Denning.

[5] See *ibid., per* Russell, L.J.

Finally, section 147 continues:

"(4) Nothing in subsection (2) of this section shall be taken to exclude or restrict any right which an employer would have apart from that subsection to dismiss (with or without notice) an employee who takes part in a strike."   **[429]**

The breach of contract, it will be noted, is still there. Even though the employer cannot sue for that breach, he may dismiss a striker, even though due notice has been given.   **[430]**

INDEX

All references are to paragraph numbers.

A

AGENCY SHOP AGREEMENT
application for, [16], [60], [225],
[230]
CIR functions in relation to, [66]
conscientious objector, [221]–[222],
[224]
contribution to trade union, [86],
[219]–[220]
failure to pay, [236]
definition, [218]
discontinuance of, [232]
discrimination against non-member of union, [366]
duty of employer in relation to, [328]
employers' failure to enter into, [16]
formation of, [225]
inducement of employer not to
observe, [283]–[286]
inducement of trade union not to
apply for, [311]
order for, [228]–[230]
periodic payments, [219]–[220]
revocation of, [17]
settlement of disputes, [223]–[224]
unfair industrial practice in relation
to, [231], [233]–[236]
unregistered organisation of employers, [159]

APPROVED CLOSED SHOP
AGREEMENT
application for, [18], [211]
approval of, [212]–[213]
CIR functions in relation to, [67]
conscientious objector, [214]
contributions to trade union, [86]
definition, [210]
discontinuance of, [19], [215]
discrimination against non-member
of union, [367]
effect of, [214]
inducement to employer to apply
for, [217], [290]
unfair industrial practice in relation
to, [216]–[217]
unregistered organisation of employers, [159], [290]

ARBITRATION
Industrial Arbitration Board. *See*
INDUSTRIAL   ARBITRATION
BOARD

ARBITRATION—*cont.*
powers of Government before Act
of 1971, [356]
procedure, [1]

C

CIR. *See* COMMISSION ON INDUSTRIAL
RELATIONS

CLOSED SHOP AGREEMENT
agency shop agreement, [209]. *See
also* AGENCY SHOP AGREEMENT
approved. *See* APPROVED CLOSED
SHOP AGREEMENT
discrimination against non-member, [369]
inducement to enter, [288]
post-entry, meaning, [208]
pre-entry—
exceptions to ban, [209]
meaning, [208]
void, [209]
unapproved, [20]

CODE OF PRACTICE
basis on which prepared, [4]
date on which comes into effect,
[45]
effect of, [5]
evidence in proceedings before
NIRC or Industrial Tribunal,
[5]
failure to observe, [5], [45]
good industrial relations, [329]
information—
disclosure of, [205]
failure to disclose, [94]
Parliament, to be laid before, [4],
[45]
preparation of, [4], [43]–[45]
purpose of, [4]
revision of, [4], [43]–[44]
timing of, [4]

COLLECTIVE AGREEMENT. *See
also* COLLECTIVE BARGAINING
breach of, [307]
construction of, [40]
contract of employment, terms incorporated in, [261], [423]–
[426]
contractual effect, [241]–[246]
enforcement, [241]–[244]
federated agreements, [241]

PRECEDENT
doctrine of, [3]
application to NIRC, [3]

PROCEDURE AGREEMENT. *See
also* COLLECTIVE AGREEMENT
absence of, [47], [247]
CIR, reference to, [50], [68]
defective, [247]
designating order relating to, [21]
dismissal under, [388]–[389]
duty to notify Secretary of State,
[334]
legally enforceable, [22]
application for, [22]
exemption from, [46]
provisions of, [22]
revocation of, [22]
meaning, [240]
notice to employee of, [403]
notification to Secretary of State,
[49], [258]
unfair industrial practice relating
to, [254]–[257]
unregistered organisation of employers, [160]
unregistered organisation of
workers, [171]

R
RACIAL DISCRIMINATION, [409]

REDUNDANCY, [60], [373]–[374],
[411]

REGISTER
provisional, [76]
cancellation of entries, [114],
[116]
effect of entry on, [77]
employers' association in, [157],
[159]
establishment of, [113]
special, [79]
application for entry in, [163]–
[164]
effect of entry in, [166]
elegibility, [161]–[163]
federated organisation, [164]–
[165]
organisation registered as company, [121]
purpose, [161]
rights of organisations in, [166]

REGISTRAR OF TRADE
UNIONS AND EMPLOYERS'
ASSOCIATIONS
administrative powers, [82]–[83]
appeal against decision of, [32]

REGISTRAR OF TRADE
UNIONS AND EMPLOYERS'
ASSOCIATIONS—*cont.*
complaint against employers'
association to, [80], [158]
disclosure of evidence before, [10],
[379]
functions, [2], [75]–[83]
inspection of documents, [60]
investigation of complaints, [30],
[106]–[108], [111]
investigatory powers, [80]–[81],
[158], [338]
NIRC—
complaint to, [31]
powers exercised through, [27]
powers of, [75], [80]–[81], [158],
[338]
report, [74]
unfair industrial practice, [104]–[111]
winding up, application for, [122]

REGISTRATION
certificate, issue of, [78]
organisation of employers, [153]–
[160]
cancellation of, [157]
elegibility, [155]
organisation of workers—
advantages of, [123]
application for, [78], [117]–[119]
cancellation of, [28], [29], [78],
[120]–[121]
certificate of, [76], [78], [114],
[117]
effect of, [115], [117]
eligibility for, [112], [114]
refused, [32], [78]

RESTRAINT OF TRADE
not unlawful, [102]

S
SECRETARY OF STATE
ballot, application for, [52], [73]
CIR, references to, [50]
claims to be reported to, [61]
Code of Practice prepared by, [4],
[43]–[45]
collective bargaining, powers in
relation to, [47]–[48], [50]
conciliation officers, appointment
of, [54]–[58]
"cooling off" order, application
for, [52], [73], [347]
discrimination, powers in relation to, [59]
emergency procedure, powers in
relation to, [347], [350], [351],
[354]